wicazō ṡa review

A Journal of Native American Studies

Editor
Lloyd L. Lee, University of New Mexico

T0309958

Associate Editor
Amy Lonetree, University of California, Santa Cruz

Book Review Editor
Madeline Rose Mendoza, University of New Mexico

Founding Editors
Elizabeth Cook-Lynn
Roger Buffalohead
Beatrice Medicine
William Willard

Contributing Editors
Majel Boxer, Fort Lewis College
Duane Champagne, University of California, Los Angeles
Steven J. Crum, University of California, Davis
Ellen Cushman, Michigan State University
Clayton Dumont, San Francisco State University
Donald Fixico, Arizona State University
Lawrence Gross, University of Redlands
Suzan Shown Harjo, The Morning Star Institute
Tom Holm, University of Arizona
Ted Jojola, University of New Mexico
Glenabah Martinez, University of New Mexico
Cornel Pewewardy, Portland State University
Lisa Poupart, University of Wisconsin, Green Bay
Kathryn Shanley, University of Montana
Luci Tapahonso, University of New Mexico
Laura Tohe, Arizona State University
Edward Valandra, University of South Dakota, Vermillion
Michael Yellow Bird, Humboldt State University

WICAZO SA REVIEW • SPRING & FALL 2020,
VOL. 35, 1 & 2

CONTENTS

Reviews

Editor's Commentary

Lloyd L. Lee

Yá'át'ééh! I hope everyone is doing well. Our volume 35 is a combined edition of number 1 and 2 with four articles, one literary essay, one commentary, and six book reviews. In 2022, we resumed the publication of the journal with volume 34, number 1 (spring 2019) and number 2 (fall 2019). We are now in the process of making sure we catch up with editions being released as soon as possible. With this combined volume 35, number 1 and 2 (spring/fall 2020) edition, we anticipate four editions (volume 35 [2020], 36 [2021], 37 [2022], and 38 [2023]) being released in 2023 and early 2024. It is my goal to be caught up by 2024. We know numerous and important articles, essays, commentaries, and reviews will be forthcoming in the editions and we want to make sure Native Nations and Indigenous peoples' sovereignty, integrity, cultures, and identities are protected and sustained.

In this thirty-fifth edition, the articles display a variety of topics, an engaging literary essay, a thought-provoking commentary, and some insightful reviews on recent released books.

The first article, cowritten by Sarah Hernandez and Kendall Tallmadge and titled "#NativeReads: Outcomes of an Oceti Sakowin Survey and Literary Recovery Model," details an example of how Native Nations and Indigenous peoples can define and articulate their own literary traditions. In the state of South Dakota, new social studies standards have removed references to the Oceti Sakowin ("The Seven Council Fires" or Dakota, Nakota, and Lakota nations). This erasure and attempt to prevent Oceti Sakowin students from learning about their own ways of life and communities and ensuring all of the South Dakota student population remains ignorant is dangerous and troublesome. Hernandez and Tallmadge's article discusses a new educational resource designed and led by the community that represents how Indigenous peoples are empowering and reclaiming control of their own long-standing intellectual traditions to share knowledge and wisdom for future generations.

The second article, "'She Likes Fish Camp': Legal History and Alaska Native Subsistence Practices in Diane Lxéis Benson's play *River Woman*" by Thomas Michael Swensen, examines how state and federal laws focusing on land and subsistence rights in Alaska worked to disempower the character River Woman in the play and Alaska Native peoples overall. The article reviews the legal history that led to land ownership and tenure in Alaska, subsistence rights, the Homestead Act of 1862, the Alaska Native Claims Settlement Act of 1971, and US government policies leading to dire consequences for the character River Woman and Alaska Native families. The article also brings to the forefront Alaska Native land dispossession oral narratives. The narratives show the resistance and continuation of River Woman and the Alaska Native peoples.

The third article, "'Disability' through Diné Relational Teachings: Diné Educational Pedagogy and The Story of Early Twilight Dawn Boy" by Sandra Yellowhorse, discusses "disability" from an Indigenous perspective. Yellowhorse focuses on Diné relational principles embedded in a Diné educational pedagogy; a distinctive lifeway and model of living for Diné peoples. She retells the story of a Diné narrative to display an understanding of "disability" based on Diné lifeways and intellectual traditions. The narrative is a lens into seeing other ways of being grounded in place, community, and belonging. This sense of knowing and being illustrate Indigenous ways, perspectives, and understandings regarding life.

The fourth article, by Heather J. Shotton and Robin Zape-tah-hol-ah Minthorn titled "Narratives of Indigenous Women Leaders: Indigenous-Centered Approaches to Leadership," addresses the roles and realities of Indigenous women in leadership. While there is a growing literature about Indigenous women in the twenty-first century, there still remains a need for scholarship that considers the perspectives of Indigenous women and leadership. This article helps to fill the gap and address Indigenous female perspectives on the critical needs of leadership.

The literary essay titled "Using Stories to Teach" by Aretha Matt describes her personal experience of using narratives to teach. Her background and experiences have compelled her to teach colleagues and peers about her upbringing and Diné ways to prevent them from developing stereotypical perspectives and other common misconceptions of their Native students and Native peoples overall. Matt's essay is relatable as a Native scholar myself and the need to teach and educate non-Native peoples about the humanity of Indigenous peoples and the sustainability of distinct Native Nations and communities.

Jeff Rasley's "Reparations for Native American Tribes?" is an unusual commentary. Discussions in the United States about African American reparations and Rasley's *America's Existential Crisis: Our Inherited Obligation to Native Nations* brings to the discussion table a focus on Native American reparations. Rasley argues his approach can be less politically controversial. His commentary is not necessarily new to Native peoples; however, his contribution to this question might bring a new way to think of federal Indian policy and federal and state relations with Native Nations.

Along with the four articles, literary essay, and commentary, six book reviews are a part of this combined edition. The reviews are on the following texts: *Earthworks Rising: Mound Building in Native Literature and Arts* (2022) by Chadwick Allen, *A History of Navajo Nation Education: Disentangling Our Sovereign Body* (2022) by Wendy Shelly Greyeyes, *Gichigami Hearts: Stories and Histories from Misaabekong* (2021) by Linda LeGarde Grover, *Hungry Listening: Resonant Theory for Indigenous Sound Studies* (2020) by Dylan Robinson, *Red Scare: The State's Indigenous Terrorist* (2021) by Joanne Barker, and *Di-bayn-di-zi-win (To Own Ourselves): Embodying Ojibway-Anishinabe Ways* (2022) by Jerry Fontaine and Don McCaskill. The reviewers for each text are Jonathan Radocay, Kelsey Dayle John, Katrina M. Phillips, Alexa Woloshyn, Kara Roanhorse, and Sasha Maria Suarez.

Overall, volume 35 edition 1 and 2 contributes to the field of American Indian Studies/Native American Studies seeking to protect the sovereignty, ways, and identities of Indigenous peoples, communities, and Native Nations. Áhéhee'! Thank you.

AUTHOR BIOGRAPHY

Lloyd L. Lee, PhD is an enrolled citizen of the Navajo Nation. He is Kiyaa'áanii (Towering House), born for Tł'ááschíí (Red Cheeks). His maternal grandfather's clan is Áshįįhí (Salt) and his paternal grandfather's clan is Tábąąhá (Water's Edge).

He is a professor and faculty graduate director in the Department of Native American Studies at the University of New Mexico (UNM), director of the Center for Regional Studies (CRS) at UNM, and editor of the *Wicazo Sa Review* journal. He sits on the Council for the American Indian Studies Association (AISA).

He is the author of *Diné Identity in a 21st Century World* (2020), *Diné Masculinities: Conceptualizations and Reflections* (2013), coauthor of *Native Americans and the University of New Mexico* (2017), and edited *Navajo*

Sovereignty: Understandings and Visions of the Diné People (2017) and *Diné Perspectives: Reclaiming and Revitalizing Navajo Thought* (2014). His research focuses on Native American identity, masculinities, leadership, philosophies, and Native nation building.

#NativeReads
Outcomes of an Oceti Sakowin Survey and Literary Recovery Model

Sarah Hernandez and Kendall Tallmadge

In 2021, South Dakota's Department of Education removed more than a dozen references to the Oceti Sakowin ("The Seven Council Fires" or Dakota, Nakota, and Lakota nations) from the state's new social studies standards, including any specific references to the tribes' cultures, languages, histories, geographies, and governance. For instance, elementary school students are no longer required to learn Oceti Sakowin creation stories or any other information pertaining to their tribes' rich and complex oral and print literary traditions. Middle school and high school students are no longer required to learn about Oceti Sakowin land and treaty rights, and will be prohibited from studying tribal sovereignty in their civics class. South Dakota's new social studies standards will even erase all previous references to "westward expansion, the creation of the reservation system, and U.S. assimilation policies and programs."[1] Such omissions ultimately prevent Oceti Sakowin students from learning about or taking pride in their own cultures and communities, and ensure that the rest of South Dakota's student population remains ignorant of the first peoples of the land.

The fact that Oceti Sakowin students do not see themselves reflected in public educational curricula is unacceptable. This trend has had a devastating impact on Dakota, Nakota, and Lakota youth in South Dakota, where graduation rates for Native American students hover at just 54 percent (compared to 85 percent for their non-Native counterparts). The South Dakota Sioux Falls *Argus Leader* reports that "during the 2018–19 school year, less than one in four Native American students in grades three to eight and grade 11 was rated as proficient in reading and writing on state standardized tests."[2] These statistics are especially troubling given the Oceti Sakowin's rich intellectual and literary traditions. Over the past 150 years, Oceti Sakowin writers have published nearly 200 books about Dakota, Nakota, and Lakota cultures, languages, histories, politics, and spirituality. However, these books are rarely taught in South Dakota schools, situated on the Oceti Sakowin's ancestral homelands. In a survey issued as part of the #NativeReads campaign in 2019, only 17 percent of Oceti Sakowin respondents indicated a teacher as the reason they knew about books authored from their own tribal communities.

Several recent studies indicate that one key to closing the achievement gap between Native and non-Native students is for teachers and schools to foster a greater sense of "belonging."[3] There are a number of ways to foster this sense of belonging, from hiring more Native teachers to incorporating Native cultures, languages, and histories into curricula and textbooks. In this article, we discuss a new educational resource, *#NativeReads: Great Books from Indigenous Communities—Stories of the Oceti Sakowin*, a community-led project that seeks to increase knowledge of and access to the Oceti Sakowin literary tradition.[4] As part of this initiative, two Native-led nonprofit organizations—the Oak Lake Writers' Society (Society), a tribal group for Oceti Sakowin writers, and First Nations Development Institute (First Nations), a grant-making institution that supports tribes and Native organizations as they reclaim control of their own languages, cultures, histories, natural resources, and economies—have developed several educational resources for teachers and students engaging with the rich and complex Oceti Sakowin literary tradition including a literary history/timeline, bibliography, reading list, discussion guides, author interviews, and most recently a new podcast series that has been downloaded more than 75,000 times![5]

For more than 200 years, Native representations have been shaped and delivered by individuals from outside our tribal communities (e.g., missionaries, anthropologists, historians, politicians, educators, writers, filmmakers). The #NativeReads project empowers Oceti Sakowin citizens to reclaim control of their long-standing intellectual traditions so they can share that knowledge and wisdom with future generations. This article delineates the methods and processes used to design and implement this community-led, community-derived initiative so that other tribes, Native organizations, and Indigenous literary scholars can replicate these efforts in their own communities. The Society and First Nations firmly believe it is time for the citizens of sovereign nations to define and articulate their own literary traditions.

Before delving into the #Native Reads survey data, it is first necessary to provide some background information on the Oceti Sakowin ("The Seven Council Fires"). The Oceti Sakowin consist of seven tribes based on kinship, geography, and dialect, including the Mdewakantonwan (Mdewakanton), Sisitonwan (Sisseton), Wahpekute (Wahpekute), Wahpetonwan (Wahpeton), Ihanktonwan (Yankton), Ihanktonwanna (Yanktonai), and Titonwan (Teton). These seven tribal bands are categorized into three divisions known broadly according to dialect as the Dakota, Nakota, and Lakota nations. Their traditional homelands are located in the Northern Great Plains region amidst vast prairies and rolling hills situated between Mni Sota Makoce and He Sapa (i.e., the Minnesota River Valley and the Black Hills). As Sicangu Lakota scholar Edward Valandra explains, each nation is connected to a specific land base: "The first four Fires reside in the eastern part of our traditional homeland and speak Dakota. The next two Fires reside in the central portion of our homeland and speak Nakota. The last Fire resides in the western part of our homeland and speak Lakota."[6] It is important to acknowledge these geographic and dialectical differences because each tribal band possesses its own unique physical and ideological connections to land that are sustained through their oral traditions. For example, Dakota origin stories explain that their early ancestors emerged from water and sacred river sites known as bdotes.[7] Meanwhile, Nakota and Lakota creation narratives tell them that their relatives emerged from rock at sacred places located in Pipestone, Minnesota, and the Black Hills in South Dakota, respectively.[8] Each tribal band has a distinct set of oral stories that reflects their own families/communities' genealogies, cosmologies, and epistemologies.

Since time immemorial, the Oceti Sakowin have relied on oral stories, histories, songs, and traditions to sustain Dakota, Nakota, and Lakota languages, cultures, and values. Traditionally, these stories were transmitted orally—passed down from family to family, community to community, and tribe to tribe—to remind each generation of their connection to the land and each other. However, Oceti Sakowin literature has not simply been handed down from one generation to the next—from traditional Dakota oral storytellers to more modern Dakota writers and scholars. In the mid-nineteenth century, Christian missionaries intercepted and colonized the Oceti Sakowin oral storytelling tradition, transforming Dakota, Nakota, and Lakota languages and oral stories into a written form based on an English alphabetic script.[9] It took Christian missionaries nearly half a century to transcribe and translate the Oceti Sakowin's rich and complex languages. These early linguistic/literary colonization efforts eventually led to mission schools intended to "Christianize and civilize" Oceti Sakowin people.[10]

Impressed by these assimilationist schools, Congress contracted with various churches and religious organizations to establish a system of government-funded boarding schools that were militant and often abusive.[11] Indeed, the National Native American Boarding School Healing Coalition (NABS) has uncovered countless stories of Indigenous students "who suffered physical, sexual, cultural and spiritual abuse and neglect, and experienced treatment that in many cases constituted torture for speaking their Native languages."[12] Today, many Indigenous people and communities are still healing from the historical and intergenerational trauma caused by these harsh assimilationist policies.

Native American boarding schools were intended to extinguish Indigenous languages and cultures. Although many Indigenous students forgot how to speak their ancestral languages and began utilizing the colonizer's language, boarding school educators did not completely eradicate Indigenous languages and cultures.[13] One need only look at First Nations' Native Language Immersion Initiative and the National Coalition of Native American Language Schools and Programs as evidence that Indigenous languages and cultures are still alive today.[14] In some tribal communities, elders and other leaders were able to sustain their intellectual traditions by taking them "underground" and sharing them with their children and grandchildren when they returned from boarding school. Unfortunately, however, this approach was the exception rather than the norm. As the United States intended, few boarding school students were able to retain their ancestral languages, and often had no other choice than to use the colonizer's language to preserve and perpetuate their oral stories and intellectual traditions.

In *Recovering Native American Writings in the Boarding School Press*, American literary scholar Jacqueline Emery argues that many boarding school students learned to adapt the English language and the printing press "as a powerful tool for writing against cultural erasure and for serving the interest of [their tribal] communities."[15] For example, Oceti Sakowin boarding school writers such as Charles Eastman (Santee Sioux), Nicholas Black Elk (Oglala Lakota), Luther Standing Bear (Sicangu/Oglala Lakota), Zitkala Sa (Yankton Sioux), Ella Deloria (Yankton Sioux), and Josephine Waggoner (Hunkpapa Lakota), to name but a few, adapted the colonizer's language to publish countless books that helped honor and celebrate their tribal nations, while also critiquing the United States for the harm they inflicted on Dakota, Nakota, and Lakota people and communities (e.g., war, boarding schools, religious indoctrination, allotment, relocation, termination).[16]

Today, many contemporary Oceti Sakowin writers and scholars, such as Elizabeth Cook-Lynn (Crow Creek Sioux), Virginia Driving Hawk Sneve (Rosebud Sioux), Layli Long Soldier (Oglala Lakota), Joseph Marshall III (Rosebud Sioux), Delphine Red Shirt (Oglala Lakota), and Gwen Westerman (Sisseton Wahpeton Oyate) are also following in the footsteps of early Dakota, Nakota, and Lakota oral storytellers and historians by using language to remind their people of their connection to the land and each other. Oceti Sakowin peoples have long used various traditional mediums to share their stories and histories, including winter counts, petroglyphs, dance, and song. Contemporary "Oceti Sakowin authors come from a long writing tradition, dating back to at least the 19th century," says Lakota scholar Nick Estes (Kul Wicasa), one of the writers included in the #NativeReads top ten reading list. "So we've been writing and telling our own stories for over two centuries now."[17]

Although Oceti Sakowin writers have published more than 200 books over the past two centuries, many general readers (both European American and Indigenous) are still under the misguided notion that Indigenous literatures are extinct and/or irrelevant oral traditions. To combat these misconceptions, American Indian/Native American/Indigenous literary scholars began using nationalist literary methodologies in the late 1990s/early 2000s to recover and engage anew with their tribe's literary traditions. Over the past three decades, nationalist literary scholars have published numerous books of literary criticism that attempt to situate Native American literary production into a tribally specific context, such as Robert Warrior's *Tribal Secrets* (1994), which concentrates on Osage and Dakota intellectuals. Warrior's book was soon followed by Jace Weaver's *So the People Might Live* (1997) and Daniel Heath Justice's *Our Fire Survives the Storm* (2006), which both honor and celebrate the Cherokee literary tradition; Craig Womak's *Red on Red* (1999), which focuses on the Creek Nation; and Lisa Brooks's *The Common Pot* (2008) and *Our Beloved Kin* (2018), which analyze the Wabanaki literary tradition. In recent years, Native American literary nationalist scholars have started to focus more attention on Dakota literature including Penelope Myrtle Kelsey's *Tribal Theory in Native American Literature: Dakota and Haudenosaunee Writing and Indigenous Worldviews* (2008) and Christopher Pexa's *Translated Nation: Rewriting the Dakȟóta Oyáte* (2019), which both consider how Dakota language and epistemologies influence modern/contemporary Dakota literatures.

Although more and more literary scholars are publishing books of literary criticism that seek to reclaim their tribe's rich and complex literary traditions, these academic books seem to be filtering down rather slowly to the community level, where they can be taught in schools and shared with both Native and non-Native students. Community-based projects and organizations such as #NativeReads, Oceti Sakowin Essential Understandings (OSEU), and the Center for American Indian Research and Native Studies (CAIRNS) are helping address this gap by providing teachers and students with the tools and resources they need to better understand Oceti Sakowin cultures and histories.[18] #NativeReads seeks to add to both these academic and community-based

resources by focusing exclusively on Oceti Sakowin literature and surveying Dakota, Nakota, and Lakota tribal citizens to determine which
books are most important to our tribal communities.

#NATIVEREADS:
A COMMUNITY-BASED SURVEY

First Nations Development Institute initially conceived of
#NativeReads as an initiative to promote the voices of American Indian/
Native American/Indigenous writers. In 2016, First Nations worked
with Debbie Reese, PhD (Nambé Pueblo), the founder of American
Indians in Children's Literature, to identify a list of "30 must-read"
children's books.[19] In 2019–20, First Nations launched a new iteration
of #NativeReads with Sarah Hernandez, PhD (Sicangu Lakota), assistant professor of Native American literature at the University of New
Mexico, to curate a new list of recommended books that focus exclusively on the Oceti Sakowin. Hernandez, who served as the Society's
executive director at the start of this project before transitioning to
the board, convened a #NativeReads selection committee composed
of Society members to review thirty Oceti Sakowin books and narrow them down to a top ten list of recommended readings by Dakota,
Nakota, and Lakota writers.[20]

In order to identify this top ten, First Nations and the Society
surveyed forty Oceti Sakowin tribal citizens in May 2019 about their
knowledge of and access to books by writers from their own tribal
communities. From these survey results, an extensive list of nearly
200 books by Dakota, Nakota and Lakota writers was compiled. First
Nations and the Society then narrowed down this lengthy bibliography to thirty books for the #NativeReads selection committee to read
and review. From these thirty books, the #NativeReads selection committee identified ten books that are critical and foundational to understanding the Oceti Sakowin.[21] While the top ten recommended
books by Oceti Sakowin authors and the full list of nearly 200 Oceti
Sakowin–authored books have been shared and widely publicized, full
results from this community-based survey have not.

Negative stereotypes and singular narratives have long been an
issue plaguing Native communities. This issue is compounded by a
general lack of knowledge about the resources and tangible narratives
that exist about Native peoples. The #NativeReads campaign seeks to
directly challenge these stereotypes and mis-narratives by bringing
awareness to the complex and rich literary history of the Oceti Sakowin
peoples. By surveying tribal members, specifically tribal members representing their own literary traditions, citizens of sovereign tribal nations could define and articulate their literary traditions on their own
terms. Although the sample size for this survey was relatively small at

forty respondents, analyzing this data can provide additional insight and understanding to barriers and challenges for accessing Oceti Sakowin literatures. In addition, the survey findings also provide good insight into what community members think are important criteria for evaluating Native American literature and why it is important to support Oceti Sakowin authors and books.

Data Collection from #NativeReads Survey

In May 2019, the Society and First Nations led a survey to measure awareness of Dakota, Nakota, and Lakota literatures. In all likelihood, this small community-based survey marks the first time tribal citizens have been asked about their knowledge of and engagement with Oceti Sakowin literatures. The survey was sent to Society members along with students from South Dakota State University, Black Hills State University, and the University of South Dakota. First Nations also posted the survey on its social media sites including Facebook,[22] Twitter, LinkedIn, and Instagram, and thus received responses from tribal citizens across the country (primarily South Dakota, North Dakota, Minnesota, and Colorado) for a two-week period. The survey was launched under the name "One Book, One Tribe," the original name of the campaign. The survey asked for demographic information of survey respondents, questions to understand current access and knowledge of Oceti Sakowin–authored books, barriers or challenges to access, and personal beliefs on the value of Native-authored literatures and community values or guidelines for evaluating Native-authored books.[23]

Fifty individuals participated in the survey but for purposes of understanding Oceti Sakowin access to their own literary tradition, tribal members external to Oceti Sakowin tribes were filtered out of this analysis. Therefore, the survey data presented in this article represents forty individuals who identified themselves as Oceti Sakowin citizens. Respondents for the "One Book, One Tribe" survey represented a variety of Oceti Sakowin tribes, ages ranging from nineteen to seventy years of age, a range of geographical spread, and varying professional backgrounds. For the purposes of this article, the data presented serves to provide insight specifically on accessibility of Oceti Sakowin literatures to Oceti Sakowin peoples, potential reasons for accessibility issues, and the importance to community members of this literary tradition.

Demographic Data and Number of Books Read

Survey respondents were asked to provide their age as part of demographic information collected. Thirty-eight, or 95 percent of

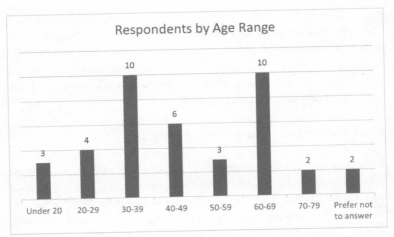

Figure 1. #NativeReads survey respondents listed by age range.

respondents, provided their age as of the date they took the survey, and two respondents preferred not to answer this question (see figure 1). When respondents were grouped into age categories by decade, the highest levels of response came from those in their sixties and those in their thirties. These respondents accounted for half of survey responses, with each of those age categories accounting for 25 percent of responses.

Survey respondents were provided with the list of nearly 200 books authored by Dakota, Nakota, and Lakota writers. When organized chronologically, Charles Eastman is the first Oceti Sakowin writer on this list to publish a full-length book in 1901. During his lifetime, Eastman published ten more books that helped pave the way for numerous other Oceti Sakowin writers. As demonstrated by this Oceti Sakowin bibliography, Dakota, Nakota, and Lakota writers have published an eclectic range of books from autobiographies and memoirs to poetry and novels to children's books and academic books from a number of different disciplines. The books on this list include writers from a variety of tribal backgrounds, experiences, and interests.

This bibliography shows the range, depth, and diversity of Oceti Sakowin writers, who write on a number of different topics and issues ranging from early Oceti Sakowin culture, language, and history to numerous contemporary issues facing our people and communities, including treaty rights, reservations, urban spaces, land stewardship and ecological knowledge, and most importantly our sovereignty. From this list, survey respondents were asked to provide the number of books they had read (see figure 2). Respondents were asked to select from one of eight bucketed categories indicating how many books they had read by an Oceti Sakowin author.

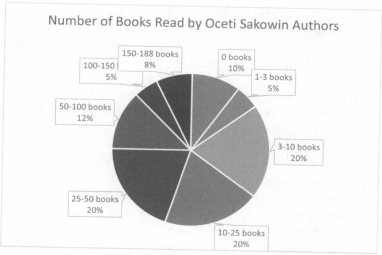

Figure 2. Number of Oceti Sakowin–authored books read by #NativeReads survey respondents.

Approximately 60 percent of respondents, or twenty-four individuals, indicated they had read anywhere from three to fifty books by Dakota, Nakota, and Lakota authors, with 20 percent or eight respondents selecting the three to ten range, ten to twenty-five range, and twenty-five to fifty range, each. The next highest range of responses was 12.5 percent or five respondents for the fifty to one hundred range. Only 12.5 percent of respondents, or five individuals, indicated reading one hundred or more books from the list and 15 percent of respondents, or six individuals, indicated reading three or fewer books on the list.

It is also important to note that four respondents said they had not read any books by a writer from their own tribal community. We suspect this number might actually be higher because individuals who had never read a book by an Indigenous writer were reluctant to take this survey. One of the respondents who had never read a book by a writer from their tribal community said they never read these books or engaged with these writers "because the[se] books are not taught in school." The other two respondents noted that "People need to be aware of these writers" and that it is important to teach these books because "It's my people," "Dakota, Lakota, and Nakota [people] finally have a voice, the real story should be told!"

The only age category to have read 150 or more books were respondents in their sixties. More than likely, this is simply an indicator of the time and research required over the years to identify and access these books. In looking further at respondents who indicated they had read fifty or more books, these individuals tended to be in higher education. Seven out of the ten respondents who had read fifty or more books indicated that they were current or retired professors or educators when asked about their occupation. Other demographic data such as geographic location and tribal affiliation did not appear to have as strong of an influence on the number of books read. However, this baseline data indicates that both profession in higher education and age of respondent contribute to the likelihood of having identified and read books by Oceti Sakowin authors.

According to these survey results, Oceti Sakowin teachers make the greatest effort to seek out books by writers from their own tribal communities, and presumably share these books with their students, who can then themselves engage with these books in meaningful and culturally relevant ways. #NativeReads selection committee member and retired educator Lanniko Lee says, "Native American teachers are excellent role models. They have cultural knowledge. They value the importance of Indigenous history, language, geography, and sovereign citizen responsibilities that every Native American student needs to develop a healthy self-identity."

Barriers to Access

Teachers are critical to promoting the Oceti Sakowin literary traditions; and yet they are not sharing Dakota, Nakota, and Lakota authors and books regularly in their classrooms. As part of the #NativeReads survey, we asked Oceti Sakowin tribal citizens how they heard about Dakota, Nakota, and Lakota books. Survey respondents were provided the following options for response to this question: Family member, teacher, friend, self, or other. Thirty-six of the forty individuals surveyed provided an answer to this question. The four respondents who had not read any of these books did not answer this question. More than half of those who responded to this question, or 58 percent of responses received, selected self as the person who recommended and/or assigned these books. The next highest category was family member, friend, or other at approximately 25 percent. Surprisingly, or perhaps unsurprisingly, only 17 percent of respondents indicated that teachers recommended these books to them.

Overwhelmingly, this information highlights the lack of general awareness of Dakota-, Nakota-, and Lakota-authored books, with many individuals needing to gather and seek out this literary tradition on their own. This data is supported by anecdotal evidence from many members of the #NativeReads selection committee and Oak Lake Writers' Society, who note that teachers rarely recommended Dakota, Nakota, and Lakota books to them in school. Even Oceti Sakowin writers who appear on the #NativeReads top ten list note that it was rare for them to read or discuss Dakota, Nakota, and

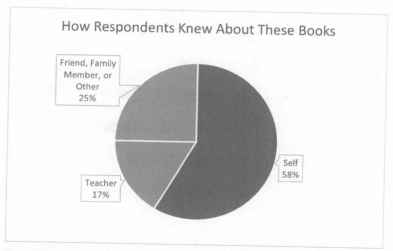

Figure 3. Primary recommender to survey respondents about Oceti Sakowin–authored books.

Lakota books in school. During his #NativeReads podcast interview, Sicangu Lakota author Joseph Marshall III recalls, "When I was in junior high and high school, I never heard about Native writers so it was disappointing to me." He says when he got older and began reading writers from his own tribal community such as Virginia Driving Hawk Sneve (Sicangu Lakota) and Luther Standing Bear (Oglala Lakota), he started to think to himself, "If they can write a book, maybe I can too."[24] Oceti Sakowin students deserve to see themselves and their communities positively represented in their classrooms and textbooks. These representations not only have the potential to instill cultural pride and values, they also have the potential to inspire a new generation of Dakota, Lakota, and Nakota writers and storytellers. Often, however, it is difficult for Oceti Sakowin citizens to even access books by writers from their very own tribal communities. In a survey issued as part of the #NativeReads campaign in 2019, only 17 percent of Oceti Sakowin respondents indicated a teacher as the reason they knew about books authored from their own tribal communities (Figure 3).

Finally, survey respondents were asked what barriers they experienced trying to access these books. Survey respondents could select from the following options:

- You did not know about these books
- They were not taught in schools
- They are not available in the library/bookstore
- They are out of print
- Other

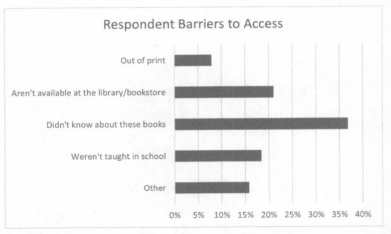

Figure 4. Primary barriers to access of Oceti Sakowin–authored books as identified by #NativeReads survey respondents.

Thirty-eight of the forty individuals surveyed responded to this question. No information was provided for the reason two individuals did not respond to this question. Respondents were only able to select one primary answer to this question, although multiple barriers to access may have existed. Approximately 37 percent of respondents who answered this question indicated that the main barrier to access was not being aware of these books. This was followed by approximately 21 percent of respondents indicating these books were not available at a library or bookstore and approximately 18 percent of respondents indicating these books were not taught in schools. Approximately 16 percent of respondents selected other, meaning that their barrier to access was not listed, and approximately 8 percent indicated it was because the books were out of print.

Accessing Oceti Sakowin books was not only difficult for survey respondents but also for the #NativeReads selection committee, all of whom live in South Dakota. The committee reported having difficulty finding books by Dakota, Nakota, and Lakota authors in their local libraries. Further, when First Nations purchased some of these books from publishers they were delayed as many were print on demand, meaning publishers do not print these books until somebody purchases them. Such barriers underscore the difficulty of accessing books by Dakota, Nakota, and Lakota writers even within their own ancestral homelands.

Shifting Importance of Teachers in Barriers to Access

Although these barriers to access again indicate a lack of representation and awareness of Oceti Sakowin literatures, one insight from the survey responses points to the role of education in disseminating this type of knowledge. The survey respondents who selected teacher as the individual who recommended and/or assigned these books were all in their thirties or younger. This could serve as a positive indicator that these books are now being incorporated into curricula and are becoming more widely disseminated as part of higher education than in the past.

Though small in sample size, five of the six respondents who selected the teacher option resided in South Dakota and the remaining respondent resided in New Mexico. These are both states in which education content recommendations are provided for history and culture of local Indigenous communities. For now, the South Dakota Department of Education provides "Oceti Sakowin Essential Understandings and Standards" with recommendations dating back to 2012 and revised recommendations posted in 2018. Meanwhile, New Mexico incorporates education on Native history and culture primarily into its K–12 social studies standards.

Teachers have the potential to increase knowledge and awareness of the Oceti Sakowin literary tradition. However, South Dakota, like many states around the country, has difficulty recruiting and retaining Native teachers who can help share information about Native cultures, histories, and literature. Further, South Dakota does not have mandatory curricula on Oceti Sakowin education and new revisions could threaten and reduce current recommended content standards. The state's Department of Education website indicates that content standards "serve as expectations for what students should know and be able to do by the end of each grade." These standards do not "mandate a specific curriculum."[25] In fact, several bills requiring Oceti Sakowin education to be taught in schools failed as recently as May 2021[26] and February 2022[27] despite statewide polling that indicated many South Dakotans supported teaching Native history and culture. Furthermore, working revisions to content standards in 2021 have further reduced references and incorporation of Oceti Sakowin history and culture.[28] At the time of this writing, the South Dakota Department of Education announced the formation of a new Social Studies Commission in April 2022 that is tasked with reviewing the new standards before they are approved and open for public comment.[29]

Community Values and the Importance of Native Authors

When asked why it was important to support Oceti Sakowin authors, survey respondents provided a wide variety of answers ranging from historical lack of representation to truth-telling and general education of Native cultures and histories. In fact, many of these responses reflected data previously collected under the Reclaiming Native Truth

(RNT) project. One key finding from RNT unveiled the popular romanticization of Native peoples as rooted in the past, which subsequently renders contemporary Native peoples invisible.[30] Survey respondents shared these sentiments in answering why it was important to support Oceti Sakowin authors. Many survey respondents noted the lack of awareness, visibility, and promotion of Native authors and Native-authored books. One respondent directly stated, "We're primarily invisible. I even did not know how many writers/literature there was [until this survey]." Tying into this sentiment was the need to share Native narratives to combat stereotypes and share stories of modern Native America. Promoting Native authors aids in truth-telling and sharing much-needed perspectives about lived history and cultures.

Last, survey respondents pointed to the existing history and traditional values of Oceti Sakowin literatures as another reason to promote Oceti Sakowin authors. Many respondents shared that storytelling itself is an inherent part of Oceti Sakowin culture. Publishing written works is just one component of this long-standing tradition. More importantly, however, as demonstrated by the list of nearly 200 Oceti Sakowin–authored books, Oceti Sakowin peoples already have a strong voice and history in written literary tradition. Those voices deserve to be heard. These statements can also be tied to promising strategies offered under RNT to change public perception and the dominant narrative of Native peoples in the United States. Data gathered under RNT indicated a desire by Americans for more accurate history of Native peoples, a deep respect for Native values, and a want for increased educational opportunities about Native history and culture.[31] While Americans wish to learn more about Native history and culture, National Congress of American Indians' landscape analysis of America's schools suggests that one of the "main barriers to Native American education content in curriculum" is a lack of teacher resources and professional development opportunities.[32] #NativeReads provides educators with the resources they need to bring Indigenous cultures, histories, and literatures into the classroom. #NativeReads selection committee member Gabrielle Wynde Tateyuskankan emphasizes that "#NativeReads is an important means to correcting what has been missing in the education of all citizens in America."[33]

#NATIVEREADS: RECOMMENDATIONS AND LESSONS LEARNED

The Oak Lake Writers' Society identified five key criteria for evaluating Oceti Sakowin literature based on the survey responses received. Therefore, all books recommended as essential reading as part of the #NativeReads campaign were vetted and fit the following criteria:

Authenticity—the author must be a citizen of an Oceti Sakowin nation. Coauthored texts are not eligible for consideration.

Intergenerational Transfer of Knowledge—books must impart Oceti Sakowin culture, language, history, and social values.

Sovereignty—books must protect and defend tribal sovereignty and homelands.

Challenges Stereotypes—books must not romanticize, sensationalize, exploit, or further oppress Oceti Sakowin citizens.

Accessible and Readable—books must still be available in print. Books must be accessible to a broad audience.

With the information gleaned from this community-based survey, the Society and First Nations developed a number of important tools and resources for teachers and students. In addition to publishing a twelve-page educational booklet about the Oceti Sakowin literary tradition, several online resources were also created including a literary timeline, bibliography, recommended reading lists, discussion guides, author interviews, and a podcast series. Resources for the #NativeReads campaign are housed across both the Society and First Nations websites as well as the Red Nation's podcast series. Although First Nations' direct mail campaign promoting #NativeReads: Stories of the Oceti Sakowin has ended, the Society continues to update #NativeReads resources through their website, including the #NativeReads list of 200 books published on their website as the Oceti Sakowin Bibliography Project, which the Society can add to as more and more Dakota, Nakota, and Lakota writers continue to publish. Eventually, the Society hopes to expand the #NativeReads recommended essential readings into a comprehensive website that provides educational resources on all 200 books within the Oceti Sakowin literary tradition (e.g., discussion guides, podcast interviews, lesson plans, and culturally relevant activities).

As part of our goals for promoting Native literary traditions, we would like to share recommendations and lessons learned from this project that may assist and inspire other tribes and Native organizations working toward similar efforts to reclaim their own literary traditions. Obviously, all survey participants should be Indigenous because we firmly believe it is time for tribal citizens to determine how their narratives are told. In the past, boarding school teachers determined what we read about ourselves and our communities. This trend continues today with many non-Indigenous teachers and administrators determining core curriculum standards. Today, Indigenous teachers represent less than 0.5 percent of the teachers in America's K–12 schools.[34]

The #NativeReads survey shows that Oceti Sakowin teachers and educators tend to read the most books by writers and scholars from their tribal communities and can presumably share this information with their students.

First and foremost, when launching #NativeReads, it is important that the campaign reflects the needs and interest of the community; therefore, conducting an assessment aimed at understanding community knowledge of their own literary traditions is essential for both engaging Oceti Sakowin citizens and establishing a baseline of knowledge. For #NativeReads, this was accomplished by conducting the "One Book, One Tribe" survey. Due to time constraints, the survey was only open for three weeks. Efforts were made to promote the survey on social media. Gift cards were also offered in exchange for participation; however, these incentives were not enough to substantially increase the survey response. This could be due to a number of factors such as the limited dates of the survey, the fact that online surveys are easy to scroll by and ignore, and that people may be reluctant or hesitant to take these surveys if they have never read a book or are not aware of Native authors in their community. To combat low response rates, we recommend administering the survey in-person at a community gathering and encouraging everybody to participate in the survey regardless of whether they have read a book by an author from their community or not so you can start to examine who has and has not read these books and why.[35] In many cases it may be because these books are not taught in school or otherwise easily accessible. It is important to gather this data to see where the American school system is failing and determine additional barriers to access.

Second, we recommend administering the survey to a diverse population that represents different ages, genders, education, careers, and so on. This data will reveal trends to better address the needs of individuals within your community.

Third, we recommend convening an advisory committee to adapt and modify the #NativeReads evaluation criteria or develop independent criteria based on community feedback. The criteria shared in this article reflect the needs and interests of Dakota, Nakota, and Lakota people. Criteria utilized may and will likely vary across different tribal communities.

The #NativeReads committee had to work quickly to meet the goals and deadlines for marketing and sharing the campaign. They used the "One Book, One Tribe" survey data to narrow down the original list of 200 Oceti Sakowin books to twenty books, and then read those twenty books over a three-month period, evaluating them using the #NativeReads selection criteria (i.e., authentic, intergenerational transfer of knowledge, promotes sovereignty and self-determination, challenges stereotypes, and is accessible). The #NativeReads committee discussed these books over the phone and via email every two weeks. Fortunately, the #NativeReads selection committee was composed of avid readers who read their assigned books in one to two weeks. Instead of one to two books per week, we recommend reading and discussing one book per month to give committee members time to read and think about these books critically. The #NativeReads selection committee primarily discussed these books over the telephone due to limited time and budget constraints; however, in-person discussions would have been preferable. These discussions were informal (i.e., no preplanned questions), but developed organically and were thought-provoking because the selection committee was composed of elders and retired educators who helped guide these conversations. These discussions informed much of the content for the #NativeReads educational booklet, website, and podcast series. It is worthwhile to take notes or record these types of discussions for further reflection and future use.

In the future, we recommend that individuals wishing to replicate this model ask their selection committee members to incorporate the following questions into their discussion: What are some unique qualities or characteristics about your tribe's literary tradition? How is your oral tradition similar to or different from your print tradition? What are the most important lessons you hope future generations will take away from your tribe's literary tradition? How do these books promote or challenge these lessons? How do these books challenge or reinforce stereotypes about your tribe? Overall, how do these books impact readers' perception of your people, communities, and nation?

We recommend ordering books in advance when possible since Native-authored books can be difficult to access when those books are out of print, print on demand, or unpublished manuscripts buried in archives. The Society focused on books that were immediately accessible per the campaign's goals and criteria. Unfortunately, this excluded some authors and books from consideration. Books that are printed on demand can also be more expensive and take longer to obtain since publishers wait until a buyer orders a copy to publish them. We recommend identifying and ordering your books sooner rather than later.

Finally, we strongly recommend paying the selection committee honorariums. Many members of the selection committee would have volunteered their time and energy to assist with this project because they sincerely believe that Dakota, Nakota, and Lakota students deserve to see themselves and their communities positively reflected in their classrooms and textbooks. However, it is important to pay tribal elders and leaders for their time and expertise.

The Society and selection committee worked with First Nations staff and consultants[36] to write the content for the #NativeReads brochure and website and design the educational booklet. First Nations works closely with tribal communities to finalize all reports and published materials per its institutional and research policies. Therefore, the Society, as the community-based partner, had final say over all materials released as part of this campaign and is now working to expand the Oceti Sakowin top ten list into an interactive website for teachers and students that focuses on all 200 books within the Oceti Sakowin literary tradition.

CONCLUSION

Obviously, literature and poetry can never replace the knowledge and wisdom of tribal elders nor is that the intention of the #NativeReads campaign. Over the past 200 years, however, writing has become an important medium for Indigenous historians and storytellers to preserve and perpetuate their own cultures and histories for future generations. Unfortunately, Indigenous teachers represent less than 0.5 percent of the teachers in America's K–12 schools, and many non-Indigenous teachers are still unaware that Indigenous people have their own literary traditions. As a result, younger generations are clearly struggling to learn about and even access books and resources about writers from their own tribal communities. According to 39 percent of the Oceti Sakowin individuals surveyed as part of the #NativeReads campaign, these tribal members never even knew that Oceti Sakowin books—or in other words, the Oceti Sakowin literary tradition—existed. "There is a disconnect between generations," says Tateyuskanskan. "It's nobody's fault because that's what colonization does—it makes you fearful that your way of thinking is wrong. Because of colonization, our young people don't always know what tradition is. It was stolen from them—stolen culture, stolen language, stolen spirituality. That's why these books are so important."

The American education experience for most students is determined by a core curriculum determined by state standards for public institutions. According to RNT, 72 percent of Americans believe it is necessary to make significant changes to the school curriculum on Native American cultures and histories.[37] Although many teachers agree with these findings, they seem to lack the knowledge and experience needed to make curricular improvements. Community-based campaigns like #NativeReads provide educators with the tools and resources they need to bring Indigenous cultures and histories into the classroom.

The fact that Dakota, Nakota, and Lakota people have a long-standing literary history and do not see themselves reflected in public educational curricula and do not have regular access to their own literature is unacceptable. It has had a devastating effect on tribal youth and their communities.[38] While states like South Dakota have taken small steps in the past to incorporate Oceti Sakowin culture and history into formal education, recent efforts to ban teachings such as critical race theory threaten to undo what progress has been made. The Society and First Nations hope the #NativeReads project will inspire other tribes and Native organizations to reclaim and revitalize their own literary traditions, regardless of their state's core curriculum standards.

AUTHOR BIOGRAPHIES

Sarah Hernandez (Sicangu Lakota) is an assistant professor of Native American literature and the director of the Institute for American Indian Research at the University of New Mexico. She is the author of the forthcoming book *We Are the Stars: Colonizing and Decolonizing the Oceti Sakowin Literary Tradition* (University of Arizona Press, February 2023). Women and land form the core themes of this book, which bring tribal and settler colonial narratives into comparative analysis and further advances discussion about settler colonialism, literature, nationalism, and gender. Sarah is a member of the Oak Lake Writers' Society, an Oceti Sakowin–led nonprofit for Dakota, Nakota, and Lakota writers.

Kendall Tallmadge (Ho-Chunk) is a senior program officer at First Nations Development Institute, where she works in the Strengthening Tribal and Community Institutions program area. She received her BA in anthropology from Beloit College in 2009 and her MBA and an MA in anthropology from the University of Colorado at Boulder in 2013. She currently serves on the external advisory board for the Center for Native American and Indigenous Studies at the University of Colorado at Boulder and on the editorial board for the *Public Historian*, the official publication of the National Council on Public History.

NOTES

1 Morgan Matzen, "South Dakota DOE Removed Indigenous Topics from Social Studies Standards before Final Draft," *Argus Leader*, August 10, 2021, https://www.argusleader.com/story/news/education/2021/08/10/department-education-standards-draft-removes-native-american-topics-lakota-nakota-oceti-sakowin/5540521001/.

2 Nick Lowrey, "Native American Students Left Behind by S.D. Education System," *Argus Leader*, November 22, 2019, https://www.argusleader.com/story/news/education/2019/11/22/native-american-students-left-behind-south-dakota-education-system/4269896002/.

3 For more information about Native belonging, see Shadab Fatima Hussain et al., "Conceptualizing School Belongingness in Native Youth: Factor Analysis of the Psychological Sense of School Membership Scale," *American Indian and Alaska Native Mental Health Research* 25, no. 3 (2018): 26–51, https://doi.org/10.5820/aian.2503.2018.26, and Laurel R. Davis-Delanof et al., "Representations of Native Americans in US Culture? A Case of Omissions and Commissions,"

The Social Science Journal (September 2021): 1–16, https://doi.org/10.1080/03623319.2021.1975086.

4   Download the full #NativeReads educational brochure and podcasts at https://www.firstnations.org/nativereads.

5   In mid-March 2020, First Nations mailed the #NativeReads educational booklet to their funders and grantees. #NativeReads brochures began arriving in mailboxes shortly before states began closing down because of the COVID-19 pandemic. The Society planned several in-person events to promote #NativeReads in April, May, and June 2020. Due to the pandemic, all of the Society's promotional events for #NativeReads were canceled. To promote #NativeReads and maintain safe social distancing, the Society partnered with the Red Nation, a Native-led organization in Albuquerque, New Mexico, to produce a new podcast series about Oceti Sakowin literature. This new digital platform allowed the #NativeReads selection committee to interview more than a dozen Oceti Sakowin writers and scholars about our recommended books. The #NativeReads podcast series is the Red Nation's most popular to date and thus allowed us to reach a much wider audience than we ever expected.

6   Edward Valandra, "Oyate Kin Unkajikupi Pelo," in *In the Footsteps of Our Ancestors: The Dakota Commemorative Marches of the 21st Century*, ed. Waziyatawin Angela Wilson (St. Paul, MN: Living Justice Press, 2006), 179–191, at 191.

7   For Dakota tribal land narratives, see Gwen Westerman and Bruce M. White, *Mni Sota Makoce: The Land of the Dakota* (St. Paul, MN: Minnesota Historical Society, 2012).

8   For Lakota tribal land narratives about the Black Hills, see Craig Phillip Howe and Kimberly Tall Bear, eds., *This Stretch of River: Lakota, Dakota, and Nakota Responses to the Lewis and Clark Expedition and Bicentennial* (Brookings, SD: Oak Lake Writers' Society, 2006), and Craig Phillip Howe, Lydia Whirlwind Soldier, and Lanniko L. Lee, eds., *He Sapa Woihanble: Black Hills Dream* (St. Paul, MN: Living Justice Press, 2011). For Nakota tribal land narratives about Pipestone, see "Pipestone: The Rock," National Park Service, accessed February 8, 2022, https://www.nps.gov/nr/travel/pipestone/rock.htm.

9   For more information about how Christian missionaries transcribed and translated Dakota, Nakota, and Lakota languages and oral stories to the English language, see Stephen Return Riggs, *Mary and I: Forty Years with the Sioux* (1887; repr., Minneapolis: Ross and Haines, 1969). Also see Jacqueline Fear-Segal, *White Man's Club: Schools Race and the Struggle of Indian Acculturation* (Lincoln: University of Nebraska Press, 2007) and Linda R. Clemmons, *Conflicted Mission: Faith, Disputes, and Deception on the Dakota Frontier* (St. Paul, MN: Minnesota Historical Society Press, 2014).

10   "Our New Suit," *Iapi Oaye* (Greenwood, Dakota Territory), January 1, 1873, 4, https://www.mnhs.org/newspapers/lccn/sn95063058/1873-01-01/ed-1/seq-1.

11   Nicole Adams, Tashina Etter, and Sarah Hernandez, "Relationships, Respect and Revitalization: Grantmaking Strategies—A Guide for Native American Education and Philanthropy. Observations from a Grantmakers for Education Member Briefing, February 2006," Grantmakers for Education,

February, 2006, https://files.eric.ed.gov/fulltext/ED527094.pdf, 7.

12 National Native American Boarding School Healing Coalition, "US Indian Boarding School History," accessed February 8, 2022, https://boardingschoolhealing.org/education/us-indian-boarding-school-history/.

13 A number of Oceti Sakowin writers have written extensively about their boarding school experiences and efforts to extinguish their languages and cultures. See Charles A. Eastman, *From the Deep Woods to Civilization: Chapters in the Autobiography of an Indian* (Boston: Little Brown, and Company, 1920), Zitkala-Sa, *The School Days of an Indian Girl, and an Indian Teacher Among Indians* (Gloucester, UK: Dodo Press, 2009), and Lanniko L. Lee, Florestine Kiyukanpi Renville, Karen Lone Hill, and Lydia Whirlwind Soldier, *Shaping Survival: Essays by Four American Indian Tribal Women*, ed. Jack W. Marken (Lanham, MD: Scarecrow Press, 2006).

14 To learn more about First Nations' Native Language Immersion Initiative, see "Native Language Immersion Initiative," First Nations Development Institute, accessed February 8, 2022, https://www.firstnations.org/projects/native-language-immersion-initiative/, and "NALA," The National Coalition of Native American Language Schools and Programs, accessed February 8, 2022, http://www.ncnalsp.org/.

15 Jacqueline Emery, *Recovering Native American Writings in the Boarding School Press* (Lincoln: University of Nebraska Press, 2020), 2.

16 Collectively, Eastman, Black Elk, Standing, Bear, Sa, Deloria, and Waggoner published nearly three dozen books. For a list of these and other books by boarding school writers, see Oak Lake Writers' Society, "The Oceti Sakowin Oyate Bibliography Project," updated April 2020, https://www.oaklakewriterssociety.com/oceti-sakowin-oyate-bibliography-project.

17 First Nations Development Institute, "#Native Reads: Stories of the Oceti Sakowin," 2020, https://www.firstnations.org/wp-content/uploads/2020/03/NativeReads-Brochure-single-pages.pdf, 10.

18 Oceti Sakowin Essential Understandings, "WoLakota," https://www.wolakotaproject.org/introduction-to-the-oceti-sakowin-essential-understandings/, and the Center for American Indian Research, "Homepage" https://www.nativecairns.org/.

19 See First Nations' blog post about the first iteration of #NativeReads, http://indiangiver.firstnations.org/nl161112-08/.

20 This top ten list includes Joseph Marshall III's *The Lakota Way*, Ella Deloria's *Waterlilty*, Charles Easman's *The Soul of the Indian*, Josephine Waggoner's *Witness*, Vine Deloria Jr.'s *Custer Died for Your Sins*, Edward Valandara's *Not Without Our Consent*, Elizabeth Cook-Lynn's *Anti-Indianisim in Modern America*, Lydia Whirlwind Soldier's *Memory Songs*, Layli Long Soldier's *Whereas*, and Nick Estes's *Our History is the Future.*

21 The #NativeReads selection committee includes Patty Bordeaux Nelson (Sicangu Lakota), Tasiyagnunpa Livermont Barondeau (Oglala Lakota), Sarah Hernandez (Sicangu Lakota), Lanniko Lee (Mniconjou Lakota), Gabrielle Wynde Tateyuskanskan (Sisseton Wahpeton Dakota), and Joel Waters (Oglala Lakota).

22 First Nations Development Institute, "For Native American Heritage Month (in November), First Nations Development Institute Will Launch 'One Book, One Tribe'—A National Reading Campaign," Facebook, May 24, 2019, https://www.facebook.com /FirstNationsDevelopment Institute/posts /10155894443826529.

23 Survey questions included: 1. What's your tribal affiliation?; 2. What's your age?; 3. What's your occupation?; 4. How many books have you read by Dakota, Lakota, Nakota writers?; 5. Who recommended and/or assigned these books? 6. What barriers have you experienced trying to access these books?; 7. In your opinion, what are the Top 5 most important and/or impactful books ever written by a Dakota, Lakota, Nakota writer?; 8. Briefly explain why you selected these books.; 9. In your opinion, what is the most important criteria when evaluating Native American literature?; 10. Why do you think it's important to support and/or promote Dakota, Lakota, Nakota writers?

24 "The Lakota Way: A Conversation with Patty Bordeaux Nelson and Joseph Marshall III," The Red Nation / #NativeReads Podcast, episode 2, May 10, 2020, coproduced by Sarah Hernandez and Nick Estes, at 7:00–7:30, https:// soundcloud.com/therednationpod /nativereads-ep-2-the-lakota-way -w-joseph-marshall-iii.

25 South Dakota Department of Education, "Content Standards," accessed January 26, 2022, https://doe.sd.gov /contentstandards/.

26 Bart Pfankuch, "South Dakotans Overwhelmingly Support Teaching of Native American History and Culture in Public Schools," Keloland Media Group, November 14, 2021, https://www

.keloland.com/news/education /south-dakotans-overwhelmingly -support-teaching-of-native -american-history-and-culture-in -public-schools/.

27 Morgan Matzen, "South Dakota Will Go Another Year Without Requiring Certain Indigenous Education Lessons for Schools," Argus Leader, February 2, 2022, https://www .argusleader.com/story/news /education/2022/02/02/south -dakota-house-education -committee-kills-bill-oceti -sakowin-essential -understandings/9314826002/.

28 Morgan Matzen, "'Political Football' or 'Mountain Out of a Molehill'? South Dakota Officials Clash over Indigenous Education Standards," USA Today, August 12, 2021, https:// www.usatoday.com/story /news/education/2021/08/12 /south-dakota-education-social -studies-native-american-history /8096093002/. Meanwhile, states like New Mexico are also facing backlash but for the opposite reason. The New Mexico Public Education Department released proposed draft standards for its social studies standards (last re- vised in 2009, https://webnew .ped.state.nm.us/bureaus/literacy -humanities/social-studies/) to include racial identity and social justice themes. Once finalized, these standards would be implemented for the 2023–24 school year. See Cedar Attanasio, "Latest New Mexico K-12 Curriculum Controversy, Only on Zoom," Las Cruces Sun News, November 6, 2021, https://www .lcsun-news.com/story/news /education/2021/11/06 /latest-new-mexico-k-12 -curriculum-controversy -only-zoom/6317221001/.

29 "New Social Studies Standards Commission Announced and First Meeting Set for May 4," South Dakota State News, April, 22, 2022,

https://news.sd.gov/newsitem.aspx?id=30142.

30 First Nations Development Institute and EchoHawk Consulting, "Reclaiming Native Truth; Research Findings: Compilation of All Research," June 2018, www.reclaimingnativetruth.com/wp-content/uploads/2018/06/FullFindingsReport-screen.pdf.

31 First Nations Development Institute and EchoHawk Consulting, "Compilation of All Research," 13–14.

32 First Nations Development Institute and EchoHawk Consulting, "Compilation of All Research," 7.

33 Gabrielle Wynde Tateyuskanskan, interview with Sarah Hernandez, #NativeReads Selection Committee Meeting, Brookings, South Dakota, August 4, 2019.

34 See "Kaylee Domzalski, 'More than a Demographic': The Important Work of Cultivating Native Teachers," November 17, 2021, https://www.edweek.org/teaching-learning/more-than-a-demographic-the-important-work-of-cultivating-native-teachers/2021/11.

35 For more suggestions about conducting surveys and gathering data in a community setting, see First Nations' Food Sovereignty Assessments, 2017, https://www.firstnations.org/wp-content/uploads/publication-attachments/Food_Sovereignty_Assessments_A_Tool_to_Grow_Healthy_Native_Communities.pdf, 9.

36 Melvin Consulting PLLC, a Hopi-founded and -led firm located in Flagstaff, Arizona, managed the direct marketing campaign including coordinating the design and copyediting of campaign materials.

37 First Nations Development Institute and EchoHawk Consulting, "Reclaiming Native Truth, 13.

38 For more information about the ways in which South Dakota's education system is failing Oceti Sakowin students, see Lowrey, "Native American Students Left Behind."

"She Likes Fish Camp"
Legal History and Alaska Native Subsistence Practices in Diane Lxéis Benson's play *River Woman*

Thomas Michael Swensen

I am hopeful that one day we will no longer
have to struggle against the state for the right
to take care of our families in the manner my
mother and past ancestors survived.[1]
—Fred John Jr.

SPRING & FALL 2020 WICAZO SA REVIEW

River Woman commences with the stage lights going up to reveal the play's sole character, River Woman. She greets the audience by saying "Heeyyyeee. I haven't seen you folks in a long time." The opening scene acts as though the audience members are visitors entering into the woman's home. After the character River Woman welcomes them, she asks in a cheerful manner, "You getting away from that city for a little bit and come across us Indians at fish camp, huh?" Then she walks off the stage into the audience to physically greet them individually with handshakes, saying, "Its good to see you."[2] By acknowledging the audience in this friendly manner, *River Woman* makes them part of the production, thereby transforming them from onlookers in the seats of a theater to guests at the rural setting of an Alaska Native fish camp. During the play the stage and seating area are converted into an encampment called a fish camp with perhaps a fish trap and a shed, near a river where individuals stay for periods of time as they harvest seasonal fish to store for the coming year.

This beginning sets the stage for the play to confront the government's intervention in the lives of Alaska's Indigenous people. Throughout history the US government has interfered with Indigenous subsistence practices like hunting, gathering, and fishing, all of which prove necessary for Alaska Natives. Without large corporate grocery stores in most of Alaska's villages and towns, thousands of denizens, Native and non-Native, depend on these activities for a major part of their diet. In the last century and a half, however, Native subsistence rights in Alaska grew into a deeply controversial and political topic throughout the state due to particular legal developments around Alaska Native ownership of land and land use. Alaska Natives have struggled against the power of the government to regulate their lifeways since the region became part of the United States in the nineteenth century.

In the latter half of the twentieth century, Native American playwrights and performers became more active in representing on the stage the living conditions and histories of themselves and their families in North America. Shari Huhndorf writes of this period, saying "For Native playwrights and performers, drama became an important medium for redefining their own societies and histories in the context of ongoing colonialism." They brought their knowledge to the stage, and, as Huhndorf writes, "Quite expectedly, the stories they told were, for the most part, markedly different from those that had become commonplace in American theater."[3] Diane Benson's *River Woman* speaks to this by delving into the friction between Native traditions and federal law. No stranger to formal Alaska state politics, Benson has long practiced as an Alaska Native activist. She even ran as the Green Party candidate for governor of Alaska in 2006, finishing second in the statewide election.[4] This essay argues that the bundle of laws dealing with land and subsistence rights in Alaska work in concert to disempower the character River Woman.

River Woman explores what it means for an Alaska Native family to face homelessness at the hands of state and federal laws. This essay proceeds by reviewing the legal history that led to the contemporary Alaska Native land ownership and tenure crisis depicted in the play. After that discussion, I examine the subsistence rights that, aligned with land ownership, are important to the spirit of the play. Then I argue that the Homestead Act of 1862 combined with the Alaska Native Claims Settlement of 1971 contributed to the displacement of River Woman and her family. The play shows how these laws produced dire consequences when they combined with other social policies by the federal government. The final part of the essay considers River Woman's raven story as an extension of a traditional oral narrative about Alaska Native land dispossession.

Figure 1. *River Woman*'s author Diane Benson performing on stage with Chris Makua in a Naa Kahidi Theater production. Alaska State Archives. Identifier ASL-P22-26-1-1 Collection Name Alaska Division of Tourism Photograph Collection, ca. 1950-[ongoing]. ASL-PCA-22 From *Fires on the Water*, 1989, Naa Kahidi Theater [written by Dave Hunsaker (Photo by Fred Andrews).

In discussing the play, Tlingit Haida scholar Jeane Breinig emphasizes the significance of Benson's work about Alaska Native cultural experience in the twentieth century. Breinig notes that "Life's creative possibilities for transformation and renewal are . . . important to . . . Tlingit writer, Diane Benson." In that way the play serves to comment on present political conditions by converting the bereavements of Native history into the domestic lives in Alaska on a daily basis. Benson herself concurs with Breinig, noting that her work is about a process of renewal. Breinig quotes Benson who says that her work is "about pain and recovery . . . I want to move people, to cause them to experience sadness and then hope. Sometimes to laugh in the midst of despair. No matter what, hope is the outcome."⁵ Through expressing anguish and humor about dispossession, the play *River Woman* copes with the law's outcomes as it centers on the story of how a family faced legal encroachment. In Alaska, rural and village subsistence practices, like hunting, gathering, and fishing, are connected to home and family tradition as well as being deeply rooted in Indigenous traditions. In the play, Benson reveals that the disintegration of the family unit was done through a host of regulations and policies imposed from the outside. The result illustrates the prominence of intergenerational transfer of traditional knowledge from parent to child in Indigenous life.

While *River Woman* is a contemporary story, it speaks to a longer history dating back to the United States' purchase of the territory from Russia in 1867. The traditional rights of Alaska's Native peoples grew obscured through laws that promote growth based on an influx of newcomers to the impairment of Native tradition. This part of the essay reviews the nation's legal cannon that lent preference to Alaska non-Native residents in regard to land ownership and land usage. Since the 1867 Treaty of Cession between Russia and the United States, which conveyed Russia's American holdings to the young nation, land-use rights for Alaska Natives developed, unlike those of their counterparts in the contiguous United States. Hundreds of federally recognized tribal governments in the "lower 48" may possess extra-constitutional rights that allow them to hunt, fish, and gather foods on reserved and non-reserved lands. This is not the case for the members of the hundreds of tribes or villages in Alaska because the United States has refused to acknowledge such Indigenous sovereignty. Many of these aforementioned rights are based on treaties and other agreements, some of them made as the United States expanded to the Pacific shore of lower North America and others made later through congressional action or executive order when the United States recognized a nation's sovereignty. The nation purchased the Alaska territory from Russia as it was ending the treaty-making period with Indigenous nations elsewhere.

Unlike the nations below them in the United States, Alaska Natives possess no such recognized treaty rights with the United States; thus, the clarification of their uses and ownership of the land continues to unfold today. However, even though Alaska Natives are without direct agreements about their ownership, they were mentioned in the bill of sale with Russia back in 1867. The Treaty of Cession asserts, "The uncivilized tribes will be subject to such laws and regulations as the United States may, from time to time, adopt in regard to aboriginal tribes of that country."[6] In other words, the treaty proclaims that the government might at a future time treat Indigenous people—whom the government would eventually call Alaska Natives—in a similar fashion as the tribes in the contiguous part of the nation.[7]

Ninety years later in the 1960s, a movement arose from northern villages to recognize the shared interests to negotiate a set of claims with the new state and federal governments. These people of varied cultures came together because both land and subsistence living were foundational for Native communities. Decades-long litigation led to the federal government passing the Tlingit Haida settlement of 1968 while a growing movement in northern Alaska came to influence the direction of future Alaska Native–US government relations. The result of activists working with the state and federal governments was the passage of the Alaska Native Claims Settlement Act of 1971 (ANCSA), a law that treated Alaska Natives distinctly from their counterparts in the contiguous part of the United States, which in its original form gave treatment to the importance of subsistence practices. The settlement released the government to develop land for economic purposes, oil, gas, and coal without having to work with Native communities. In making an agreement with Alaska Natives, the law extinguished aboriginal title, or property rights, while never acknowledging amid the settlement process that the rights existed in any way.

In lieu of developing recognized tribal governments, the law established twelve large Native-operated regional corporations and just under 200 smaller village corporations set within the boundaries of the regionals, which had to turn profits for their Indigenous shareholders.[8] Later the federal government established a thirteenth corporation in Seattle to represent Alaska Natives who lived in the contiguous part of the nation. The subject of subsistence living remained unaccounted for in the settlement, even though the law brought forth numerous legal codes and regulations that changed Native life. The settlement lent a pause to the land ownership issue but did little to nothing to advance Alaska Native subsistence rights.[9] Robert Anderson writes that "ANCSA did not provide any statutory protection for Native hunting, fishing, and gathering rights on lands important for subsistence purposes. Some earlier versions of proposed legislation provided some protection on public and Native lands."[10] Though the corporations were intended to serve Alaska Native needs, the law left the subsistence issue unresolved for Indigenous people in the state.

Hunting, fishing, and gathering are believed to be fundamental for Alaska Native cultural persistence. The character in the play *River Woman* says just the thing when speaking of her subsistence lifestyle at the fish camp: "I got the best life there is to have."[11] The play explores the relationship she has with subsistence, a theme that imbricates with the ANCSA. After the settlement, Indigenous people endured a changed in their lifeways because the law terminated the occupational rights to the land. By and large, ANCSA changed the material relationship Alaska Natives had with the natural environment while altering Native status within the United States. A congressional rider attached to the settlement specified that the government could pull any lands they felt valuable from the settlement within ninety days of its passage as well as allowing up to 80 million acres of land to be stricken from public ownership. That rider then lent nine months for the secretary of the interior to make claims on land, and then five years for Congress to act on such lands. Yet by 1978 at the end of the five-year deadline, Congress failed to pursue these claims in Alaska and thus the provision lapsed, freeing the land from receiving any such designations.

With Congress unwilling to move forward on the settlement's rider, President Jimmy Carter decided to employ the Antiquities Act to many locations in Alaska in order to protect public lands. The Alaska National Interest Lands Conservation Act (ANILCA), passed into law in 1980, set out to proclaim lands for national public ownership. Going into effect, the law made 60 percent of the Alaska state public service lands. Title VIII of the law, entitled "Subsistence Management and Use," permitted "Alaska Natives and other rural residents" the right to hunt and fish for subsistence purposes.[12] Under this law traditional Native subsistence practices and non-Native Alaska residential hunting, fishing, and gathering held the same rights. ANILCA recognized no extra-constitutional rights for Alaska Natives even though they had lived in the region since before United States annexation. Miranda Strong writes that "more than serving as a means for survival, Alaska Natives and rural Alaskans traditionally view subsistence as a 'collective right based on sharing.' Thus, protecting subsistence traditions protects Alaska Native culture and rural Alaskans' social existence."[13] Yet with this law many saw that the clause conflicted with the state's constitution in that ANILCA treated rural and urban residents distinctly from one another. Miranda Strong writes, "With no rural priority in place, a weak subsistence priority, and nonsubsistence zones barring subsistence access, rural Alaskans face diminished subsistence access while commercial and sport interests continue to harvest fish and wildlife in nonsubsistence zones."[14] Thus, the law went on to create a three-party grievance between Native rights activists, rural residents, and people living in the state's cities and towns. The state constitution contrasted with the federal law to guarantee equal access to all members of rural Alaska.

In 1995 a legal conflict known as the Katie John case came about between the government and Alaska Native interests regarding subsistence traditions. Katie John, born in the village of Batzulnetas in 1915, lived there until 1937. The village became a portion of the Wrangell–St. Elias National Park and Preserve in 1964 and the government closed fishing to all members of the public. The state had closed the area of the village to subsistence hunting and fishing, but Katie John asserted that she should be able to hunt and fish there as her family had done for centuries. The Native American Rights Fund assisted with a series of cases correlated with the family's long-held fish camp. The legal battles slowed down in 2014, long after the writing of *River Woman*, without recognizing extra-constitutional entitlements for Native subsistence practices of Alaska's Indigenous people.

On stage, River Woman speaks about subsistence lifestyles on community life in Native Alaska. After she shakes hands with the audience, she says, "You sit down now. I got to get these potatoes done." Her cleaning a stack of potatoes on the stage actualizes the role of food

Figure 2. An Indigenous fish camp in Alaska. Alaska State Archives. Identifier ASL-P277-002-147 Collection Name Wickersham State Historic Site. (Photographs, 1882–1930s. ASL-PCA-277. Creator Merrill, Elbridge W., 1868–1929).

and community, the very theme of the play. As she discusses issues relating to her family and the land, she is establishing a sense of community with the audience with potatoes, a subsistence food, in her hands. The one-act play explicates how the settlement's aversion to doing meaningful work for subsistence has direct results on people. The laws' "gradual encroachment" harmed Native families and their traditional homelands by separating the land from cultural values.[15] That is, the conveyance of subsistence lifestyle from one generation to the next had no value in the law.

Taking place at a family fish camp on an unnamed river, *River Woman* turns to illustrate how state and federal laws come to change culture. In "Law's Territory (A History of Jurisdiction)," Richard Thompson Ford suggests of state territoriality that "we could think of a continuum between larger and smaller territorial institutions, with the family at one pole and the nation at the other."[16] In *River Woman*, the jurisdictional practices of the state establish an authoritative relationship between the natural environment at one level and the domestic space of the family on another. That is, the federal and state claims made on the land to organize it also come to affect the domestic sphere of the families that live on it.

In order to express the relationship between people and land, *River Woman* draws on the collaborative nature of theater to articulate the loss of family cohesion and destruction of the domestic sphere as part of the consequence of state and federal law. When the character brings the audience into her life, she makes them participants in the events that follow the opening scene. Through becoming part of the context of the scene they get a feel for the traditions River Woman is acting out and discussing with them.

The state's alteration of this relationship sets her into disarray. The family life depicted in *River Woman* illustrates how subsistence-based living falls victim to contrasting conceptions of land ownership, between Native cultural practices and the legal codes of state and federal governments with detrimental ramifications befalling Native individuals across generations. Native traditions of stewardship rail against Alaska state legal land tenure. Transpiring at a traditional fish camp, the play unfolds showing how Indigenous customs, in this case participating in fish camp, are not validated as a legitimate domestic tradition by Western institutions.

Many Alaska Native families possess traditional locations where they have been fishing and hunting for generations. *River Woman*'s entire play happens at the fish camp after the character appears on the stage, peeling potatoes and greeting the audience. When she touches and speaks with the audience, she breaks the fourth wall between the performance and the audience, therefore merging the dramatic space of *River Woman*'s stage with the world outside the play. This work cancels the distancing effect of alienating the audience from the actor and the storyline.[17] In making the play appear less a dramatic production and more of an event, the audience members become fellow "fish camp" inhabitants.

Following her return to the stage, the character River Woman then speaks to the audience about the past practice of harvesting vegetables in her home village. "Hey you remember how we used to get potatoes outta that garden back home," she asks, "right in the middle of the village?"[18] It is as though the audience members are fellow denizens of her village as she reveals a primary aspect of subsistence living for Native people living the rural village life in Alaska. As though the audience remembers when they too used to benefit from the communal garden. By doing this she explicates that the center point of the village was based on a custom of sharing foodstuffs cultivated collectively.

Her memories about the village life relay that she no longer lives in the village and that the fish camp where she resides was not a planned permanent home. It is but a second familial space outside the village and River Woman explains that she was forced to vacate her home. "We had a good time," she reminisces, "Before those homestead things, I guess that's what they call it."[19] When River Woman mentions these "homestead things," she is alluding that her family maybe homesteading at the camp, when in fact she is telling that they were displaced because of the state of Alaska allowing homesteading in rural regions of the state.

She unearths her recent and familial history of displacement through her reference to the federal government's Homestead Act of 1862. The Homestead Act that she cites was enacted during the Civil War, long before the late-twentieth-century setting of the play, even before the nation purchased the region now known as Alaska from Russia. She speaks of the law as though everyone in the audience would know about it. The United States enacted the Homestead Act for the initial purpose of allowing American citizens and intended citizens to claim up to 360-acre parcels of surveyed government land. The act was part of the national project to settle lands west of the Mississippi along the great plains amid the conquest of the Plains tribes. A non-Native White man of European descent occupying, for the sake of national expansion, would over time earn the ownership of the parcel. In order to gain a clear title to one of these tracts of land, a settler was required to use the acreage as a primary residence, at the very minimum a "claim shack," for five years and to cultivate the land.

Federal support for homesteading in Alaska began when President William McKinley initiated the Homestead Act of Alaska 1898.[20] Though citizens intermittently employed these acts to gain land in the mid-twentieth century, they stayed in effect until the passage of the Federal Land Policy and Management Act of 1976 in the contiguous part of the nation and later in 1988 this law fell out of practice in the state of Alaska.[21] A non-Native man named Kenneth Deardorff, who had been living in Alaska previously, was allowed by the government to file a claim for an eighty-acre plot in Stony River, Alaska, traditionally known as K'qizaghetnu Hdakaq'. He had fulfilled all requirements for the homestead by 1979 but was not able to garner title until 1988. He was the last beneficiary of the Homestead Act. His land is located in area of western central part of the state, approximately one hundred miles south of the town of Ruby, Alaska, the traditional area of Athabaskan people.[22] Thus, as River Woman discusses life before the Homestead Act, she is calling attention to its concurrence with Native dispossession.

The character River Woman then changes the subject to detail on how the Homestead Act was applied to her village. She does this by relating the law to how the Alaska Native Claims Settlement Act opened up their traditional land, perhaps even their village, for state ownership. During the formative times of the Alaska Native Claims Settlement Act, many Native village communities were to stake out tracts of land they would want to keep as part of their village or regional corporate holdings but found that they were in competition with state, federal, and private interests that also sought to own the same land. In regard to this process of land selection, River Woman tells the audience of her family's entanglement with the settlement law. She describes how her brother "didn't get some kind of paper work done or something," and due to this "the government didn't know it was his land so they took it away from him."[23] The family lost the rights to the village area land, she discloses, due to her brother's inability to file the claim with the government at the time of settlement. The government printed settlement documents only in English and not all village members spoke or read the language fluently, which caused confusion among Indigenous people throughout the state.

River Woman tells the audience that "now," after the claims settlement, "they"—the state and federal government—"got this homestead thing on 160 acres and all these people been comin' and lookin' like they won the bingo or something."[24] The state of Alaska then appropriated particular sets of lands through the settlement and opened unclaimed parcels to all citizens under a process derived from the federal homestead procedure. In the failure to file the proper claim measuring out their lands with the state government, the family had perhaps unknowingly relinquished their rights to lands, therefore passing them onto public possession along with thousands of acres throughout the state. The opening of these traditional lands led to a multitude of potential claim-stakers traveling to the area with the hopes of coming upon their own windfall homestead. These people gained from another's loss, similar to the Indian Removal Era, or the opening of the Great Plains in the nineteenth century. Alaska Natives possessed no treaties with the government, nor did they face relocation efforts to remove them to another region. Instead, the land they occupied transformed from theirs to government property. The play depicts that this is how the Homestead Act caused River Woman and her family to be displaced from the village and pushed to live at the family's fish camp.

At this point in the play, River Woman calls to children unseen and off stage in the wings to stay clear of the "fish wheel" at the river. The fish wheel has risen as competition for subsistence fishers as a notorious non-Native tool for commercial fishing that takes as many fish as possible from the mouth of a river to sell elsewhere. The fish wheel, a form of fish trap, serves as a way to dispossess people of their food. To the child she says, "You want something to do you come down and cut some fish strips for auntie. Come on now . . . You too Charla."[25] As the play's backstory evolves, the audience learns River Woman's brother left his daughter Charla to search for employment outside the area, perhaps in the town of Ruby, or even somewhere as distant as Anchorage.

This development in the play shows that the family members, without title rights to village lands, are unable to fully support themselves through the traditional means of subsistence practices. One can construe that the state of Alaska gained title to their traditional land through the settlement, dispossessing them of property, which then in time led to the breakup of the family. In fact, *River Woman's* dominant theme of state territoriality is seen extending through the loss of the village to the relationships between Native families themselves. Her brother is gone, and she is left to care for her niece. The breakdown of relationships draws attention to the flawed application of the law. If the state constitution demands equal rights for all citizens, then why did the state allow another citizen to take possession of land that other citizens had possessed since time immemorial?

Pausing from the chore of peeling potatoes, River Woman stands up to watch a raven pass across the sky. "That Raven like to get into mischief," she says.[26] After the bird flies by overhead, she begins a story that works as an allegory for acts of dispossession like the Alaska Native Claims Settlement. The tale begins at a time when she was picking up mail from her sister in Ruby. The two women, sitting on a porch, observe a construction worker leave a bulldozer at a jobsite and walk into the nearby woods to relieve himself. While the man disappeared into the woods, the sisters notice a raven landing on the work vehicle. The figure of the raven, akin to that of coyote, is a trickster. Throughout Native American literature of all forms, Raven holds meaningful insights given the story in which he appears. Raven can engage in malicious acts and good ones, all depending on his motivations at the moment.

In the play, River Woman's story employs the traditional Tlingit narrative "Raven Gives the Gift of Light," or also called, "How Raven Gave Light to the World," involving how Raven liberated the sun from a wealthy man in order to secure the sunlight for all people.[27] Before the contemporary time, the story tells, people lived in darkness with the exception of a wealthy man who held bags of varying types of light. River Woman's story within the story follows a rendition of a traditional oral narrative about Raven who, for the sake of his community, turns himself small and floats in the Nass River.[28] One day, the wealthy man's daughter consumes the Raven when she fetches a drink, becomes pregnant, and eventually births the raven as a son. Appearing as an infant to the grandfather, Raven pleads to see the collection of bags where the man keeps light. First, Raven asked to see the stars, then the moon, and finally the sun. Upon handling these bags, the Raven releases the moon and the stars as well as the sun. From this time forward, all people, not only the wealthy man, live in light.

In reference to this traditional narrative, River Woman continues her version of the story, in which Raven in Ruby pulls a chocolate bar from a box contained in the bulldozer once the construction worker has left for the woods. Her description of Raven stealing the chocolate bar is similar to how Raven took the moon, stars, and sun from the wealthy man in the traditional story. Unlike the traditional tale, however, the raven in *River Woman* places the chocolate bar on the hood of the vehicle and returns to the box for even more items. In the continued absence of the construction worker, Raven continues to liberate the sweet food in excess, stacking a total of seven bars on the bulldozer's hot hood. The bird intends to appropriate the man's chocolate without leaving him any. As the sisters watch the man return from the woods, Raven attempts to carry away all seven of the bars at once. The winged trickster drops one back onto the hood as he flies away, luckily escaping the construction worker's notice. Upon his return from the woods, the worker immediately sees the chocolate bar melting on the vehicle.[29]

Finding the stash box empty, he confronts the sisters about the theft. "We tried to tell him Raven took it, but he didn't believe us," she explains, adding, "Dat white man don't know his people just as greedy as that raven. It seems like they always think that everything belongs to them."[30] As in the traditional story, where Raven liberates the sun, moon, and stars from a covetous man, Raven in *River Woman* frees the chocolate bars from the bulldozer operator, who, as a sign of encroachment, and the privatization of land, mimics the story of the man who held all the light in various bags. Raven shows that greed is sloppy and possesses limited reason when seeking to fulfill its desire. This critique of US territoriality of Native lands through the settlement, similar to the raven's unruly desire for chocolate bars, gains even more depth as the play continues to reveal dispossession at a most intimate level.

Following this raven tale, the play makes a bitter turn in order to show how the controlling of land affects the lives of an Indigenous family. In the final segment of the play, she produces a piece of paper from her pocket and hands it to an audience member, announcing that she never learned to read English. River Woman must turn to another for interpreting written correspondence. "Who is it from?" she asks, provoking the audience member in possession of the letter to read it aloud. The audience member, now a performer in the drama, holds the letter and reads, "The Division of Family and Youth Services." In response, River Woman asks the audience member to loudly recite the letter in its entirety because her "hearing is kinda bum."[31] The audience member, taking the note in hand, reads the following letter:

> Since the documents we sent several months ago, regarding the legal guardianship of Charla Carrie Albert have not been returned, and since it has been reported that said child has been abandoned, it is hereby ordered that Carrie Charla Albert be turned over to State custody until which time it is deemed in the best interest of the child to maintain residence with an appropriate family guardian.[32]

The state's assertion of authority over Charla mirrors that of the state's acquisition of the family village land for homesteading and the losses entailed through the claims settlement. Drawn into the play, the audience member becomes the interpreter of the legal impositions of the government on Native lifeways. This is similar to how the laws governing land were written in English, leaving many Indigenous people unable to properly engage with and react to them. The initial loss of land to the state that propelled the father to leave Charla with her aunt has resulted in the acquisition of the child into state custody. The settlement's intended domestication of the perceived wildness of Alaska led to the disintegration of a Native family unit. Much like Raven with the seven chocolate bars, the settlement appropriated aspects of Native Alaska in totality. The domestic sphere, central to Native self-determination, falls victim to how legal codes and the power of the state have developed through the settlement in regard to land ownership. This part of the story references a provision in the settlement having to do with intergenerational aspects of corporate shareholding, in that shares of stock would have to be transferred because those born after December 16, 1971, would not be able to enroll in the settlement.[33]

At the end of the play *River Woman*, the sole character speaks of traditional subsistence practices as important to intergenerational relationships in Native Alaska.[34] Telling the audience about her niece Charla at the site of the family fish camp, River Woman says, "I've been taking care of her. She can cut fish real good." Teaching Charla how to prepare fish equates to helping her niece learn how to live. "She likes fish camp," she exclaims. "We have to stay here til we get our food for the winter . . . We have a good life. I got the best life there is to have." River Woman's discussion about her care of Charla highlights how traditional ways of living rely on familial relationships. The government sees the fish camp, a traditional seasonal home for this family, as an unsuitable place to raise a child. Therefore, taking her into custody means that the government is transforming Indigenous culture by harming kinship.

Originally, the Alaska Native Claims Settlement was written to deny shareholder status to those born after 1971. This part of the law was amended in 1991 to allow corporations themselves to decide if they wanted to allow new shareholders into their communities. But here in the play one can see how the lack of shareholder status can damage the intergenerational community, because younger people would not be able to gain access to the corporation until the shares are willed to them. The state seeking guardianship of Charla adds another layer of dispossession to River Woman's life. Charla becomes like the chocolate bar left on the hood of the bulldozer. The child will not learn village ways from her family or take part in the business of the corporation. River Woman's response to the letter reveals that the teaching of the subsistence part of Native culture is under fire from state authority that works in conjunction with a host of laws governing land. "You mean they are gonna take her from us?" she asks. "I been takin' real good care of her. . . . She can cut fish real good. She digs up potatoes."[35] The state's removal of Charla from the fish camp tells that the child may never finish learning to take care of herself through subsistence customs. River Woman also wishes Charla to remain with her because she needs her assistance in maintaining the fish camp. The state has broken *River Woman's* traditional domestic space that is reliant on shared workloads between generations of family members.

The state's pending custody of Charla alludes to the legal complications of Native family life before the implementation of the Indian Child Welfare Act of 1978.[36] For, as River Woman believes Charla's "best interests" are being met through her education at the camp, the state authorities label her an abandoned child in need of interventional assistance. Later, with the implementation of the Indian Child Welfare Act, authorities will secure the placement of Native children with relatives, tribal or village affiliates, or willing Native adoptive parents. However, *River Woman* reveals how it was possible before the Indian Child Welfare Act to remove a child from a secure Native home into state custody through the implementation of numerous legal tools. The Supreme Court is promising to review possible complications with the law in their fall 2022 term.

The play *River Woman* connects the laws governing land tenure with state social service practices showing a bundle of laws unraveling Indigenous self-determination. The play illustrates a series of legally codified impositions, such as the claims settlement and the Homestead Act, dislocating families. In breaking the barrier between the audience and the performance, River Woman encourages one to view how Native families and the village life intricately manifested as one community through subsistence. The state of Alaska's displacement of the family through law defines the settlement's development as a force to fracture the family. The government presents Indigenous people as incapable of providing for their own welfare and itself as the arbiter of order. This is an arrangement that dismantles Indigenous self-determination through the curtailment of intergenerational exchange. Charla embodies a target of state domestication efforts to realize the vision of domesticity inherent in the settlement process. The territorialization of land significantly connects to the state's assertion of custody rights over a child. This chain of events perhaps forever augments how subsistence practices will be carried out by River Woman's family.

As the settlement places regulations on land and people, this form of "domesticity not only monitors the borders between the civilized and the savage, but also regulates traces of the savage within itself" in the way Natives become subjects of these regulations.[37] River Woman, a figure of the domestic village space, transforms from the center of the family into a target of an enterprise bent on framing Alaskan

Indigenous cultural ways as primitive—with judicious state surveillance, discipline, and intervention—through a combination of laws governing land, people, and their customary practices. In this manner, the play deals with a crossroads of laws that end village traditions and Indigenous families themselves.

GLOSSARY OF LAWS AND COURT CASES

Alaska Native Claims Settlement Act (ANCSA), ratified as 43 U.S.C. 1601 et seq., was signed into law on December 18, 1971. The law transferred title of land to twelve Alaska Native regional for-profit corporations and close to 200 local village for-profit corporations. After the settlement another regional corporation called the thirteenth corporation was established in Seattle, Washington, for Alaska Natives residing in the contiguous United States. The corporations are distinct from tribal governments in that they operate to provide Native shareholders dividends based off their profit-making enterprises.

Alaska National Interest Lands Conservation Act (ANILCA), ratified on December 2, 1980, as STAT. 2371 Public Law 96–487, allocated federal protection to regions of land and water in Alaska.

State of Alaska v. Babbitt, 54 F.3d 549 (aka Katie John I): The court held in *Alaska v. Babbitt* in 1994 that ANILCA applied to navigable waters in Alaska.

The Homestead Act, ratified on May 20, 1862, allowed the settlement of western North American to adult citizens who were the heads of families. For a small fee the law gave 160 acres of land as long as the person stayed on the parcel for five continuous years. The law stayed in effect into the twentieth century.

AUTHOR BIOGRAPHY

Thomas Michael Swensen is an assistant professor of ethnic studies at the University of Utah. He was born and raised on Kodiak Island and is an original shareholder in the Alaska Native Claims Settlement corporations Koniag and Leisnoi Village. He is also enrolled in the federally recognized Tangirnaq Native Village, aka the Woody Island tribe.

NOTES

1 Fred John Jr., "How Katie John Whipped Alaska to Protect Native Rights," October 10, 2014, *Indian Country Today.*

2 Diane Lxéis Benson, *River Woman,* in *Alaska Native Writers, Storytellers &*

Orators, ed. Ronald Spatz, vol. 17 (Fairbanks: University of Alaska Press, 1999): 259.

3 Shari Huhndorf, "3. American Indian Drama and the Politics of Performance," in *The Columbia*

Guide to American Indian Literatures of the United States Since 1945 (Columbia University Press, 2006), 288–318, at 290.

4 This essay examines her one-act play *River Woman* that initially appeared a series of three one-act plays in 1996. The piece that became *River Woman* was drawn from a larger piece of unpublished performance work entitled *Spirit of Woman* that was performed at Anchorage's Out North Theater. This play, *River Woman*, formed into stand-alone work perhaps because, as Benson admits of the endearing aspects of playing River Woman, "I really love that character." Mike Dunham, "Seeking to 'Exemplify Woman,'" *Anchorage Daily News* (AK), December 27, 1996, H15.

5 Jeane Breinig, "Alaska Native Writers, Alaska Native Identities," University of Alaska, Anchorage Books of the year 2008–09 Supplemental Readings, accessed on July 8, 2013, http://www.uaa.alaska.edu/books-of-the-year/year08-09/supplemental_readings.cfm.

6 Treaty of Cession, 1867.

7 Make note about how the United States treated tribes at this time.

8 One of the thirteen, the thirteenth was formed in Seattle for Alaska Natives who resided in the contiguous part of the nation during the enrollment period.

9 Robert T. Anderson, "Sovereignty and Subsistence: Native Self-Government and Rights to Hunt, Fish, and Gather after ANCSA," *Alaska Law Review* 33 (2016): 187–228, 187.

10 Robert T. Anderson. "The Katie John Litigation: A Continuing Search for Alaska Native Fishing Rights after ANCSA," *Arizona State Law Journal* 51 (2019): 846–847, 860.

11 Benson, 259.

12 Public Law 96–487—Dec. 2, 1980, 94 Stat. 2371.

13 Miranda Strong, "Alaska National Interest Lands Conservation Act Compliance & Nonsubsistence Areas: How Can Alaska Thaw Out Rural & Alaska Native Subsistence Rights," *Alaska Law Review* 30 (2013): 73.

14 Ibid.

15 Roy M. Huhndorf and Shari M. Huhndorf, "Alaska Native Politics since the Alaska Native Claims Settlement Act," *South Atlantic Quarterly* 110, no. 2 (2011): 388.

16 Richard Thompson Ford, "Law's Territory (A History of Jurisdiction)," *Michigan Law Review* 97 (1999): 902.

17 This distancing effect was called Verfremdungseffekt by German playwright Bertolt Brech.

18 Benson, 259.

19 Ibid., 259.

20 Homestead Act of Alaska, 30 Stat. 409, May 14, 1898.

21 It is also important to mention the Native Allotment and Townsite Act of 1906, where village sites and other lands could be claimed and surveyed for Native communities to retain and then separate from lands that were to be appropriated by the state of Alaska and the federal government.

22 "Found: America's Last Homesteader!" The Last Homesteader-Homestead National Monument of America, National Parks Service, accessed July 9, 2013, http://www.nps.gov/home/historyculture/lasthomesteader.htm.

23 Benson, 259.

24 Ibid., 259.

25 Ibid., 259.

26 Ibid., 260.

27 Perhaps the most widely read version of this story was illustrated by Bill Reid and adapted by Robert Bringhurst. Bill Reid and Robert Bringhurst, *The Raven Steals the Light* (Seattle: University of Washington Press, 1984).

28 Shirley Kendall, "How Raven Gave Light to the World," 2009, https://www.youtube.com /watch?v=YxPIVmXAihE.

29 Benson, 260.

30 Ibid., 260.

31 Ibid., 261.

32 Ibid., 261.

33 This rule was changed in the 1980s and now corporations require a majority vote to issue stock to new shareholders. It is common in my regional corporation to issue stock to "new" shareholders.

34 James Ruppert, "Alaska Native Literature: An Updated Introduction," in *The Alaska Native Reader* (Duke University Press, 2009), 335.

35 Benson, 261.

36 Pub. L. 95–608, 93 Stat. 3071, ratified November 8, 1978.

37 Amy Kaplan, "Manifest Domesticity," *American Literature* 70, no. 3 (1998): 581–606, 582.

"Disability" through Diné Relational Teachings
Diné Educational Pedagogy and the Story of Early Twilight Dawn Boy

Sandra Yellowhorse

INTRODUCTION

This article stems from the meeting place of many different stories. I draw upon Diné ancestral story in conversation with land-based knowledge found in Diné educational pedagogy—a distinct model of *knowing* based on Diné lifeway. Placed together, I argue that Diné ancestral stories and Diné educational pedagogy convey relational ways of conceptualizing disability. By re-conceptualizing disability through the lens of relationship, I dislodge it from the prevailing trajectory in which disability is often discussed more broadly. According to Māori scholar Jill Bevan-Brown, disability is often discussed within functionalist frameworks of "biological and psychological constructs of wellness, normalcy, and deviance,"[1] or through the impacts of inaccessible, marginalizing environments that are disabling.[2] Rather than approaching disability through dominant discourses rooted in Western knowledge, I approach the teachings of "disability" through Diné ontology and intellectual pedagogy. Doing so reframes the understanding of "disability" as part of a relational system that is taught through story and mapped onto land-based frameworks. The teachings of "disability" are therefore not aligned with only functionalist views of people or environment, but rather within a relational context that promotes a system of care and reciprocity encapsulated in Diné lifeway and customs. Diné people are familiar with relational systems, such as *k'é* (positive relationships).[3] *K'é* as a relational way of knowing propels a value system based on connection aimed at caretaking all our relations. This system has been with Diné people since time immemorial. Through relational lifeways, Diné learn not only about the extent of their relationships to all life (including ourselves), but also the inherent accountability that comes with it. This sense of relationality is modeled through Diné educational pedagogy, and the ancestral stories of "disability" exist directly within this model.

This article does not seek to put forward concrete definitions of disability, nor engage in a comparative discussion of wider models of disability found in educational, medical, or social discourse. Rather, I aim to focus on Diné lifeways of *relating, knowing,* and *being,* to illuminate how those lifeways deeply influence how Diné teachings guide belonging, identity, relationship, and mechanisms for reciprocal accountability in caretaking all life. I believe these values are the foundational teachings of "disability" found within ancestral story. These teachings counter the ways that disability is often associated with an individual or as the predominate understanding of a person's identity. In my refusal to define disability within Diné ontology, I acknowledge the challenges that can arise because of the ways that society and academia promote discourse of disability as a concrete, knowable *thing.* Story becomes a powerful tool to intervene in this tendency to define and offers another approach to articulate an Indigenous understanding of disability outside the constructs of mainstream disability discourse. As Bevan-Brown argues, "if a concept of disability did exist [in Te Ao Māori], it would have been very different from today's Western concepts."[4] Similarly, Māori scholar Huhana Hickey asserts that culturally sustaining approaches to conceptualizing disability within Indigenous contexts often shifts the focus to consider wider family and community systems rather than individualized approaches to the mind and body found within Western discourse.[5]

Aligning with this foundation of moving away from Western constructs in an attempt to map them onto Diné philosophy, the theoretical focus of this article aims to unpack an understanding of "disability" located solely within Diné knowledge. I do so by placing ancestral story in alignment with the lifeway of *k'é* (positive relationships) and reading both within Diné educational pedagogy to unravel what I understand the teachings of "disability" convey. I argue that both *k'é* and Diné educational pedagogy promote a key intervention in this regard; because teachings are not focused on defining what "disability" is in a Diné context, but rather shifts focus to the relational foundations that builds communities that protect and sustain conditions to thrive. This relational foundation synthesizes the teachings of "disability" by bridging them into relationships with Diné values and aspirations for harmonious outcomes for all Diné people. The ancestral story of Early Twilight Dawn Boy is oriented toward mapping the value systems that enact accountability, care, love, and reciprocity that lead Diné people individually and collectively toward completeness.

STORYTELLING: AN ONTOLOGY OF BEING

Diné intellectual engagement teaches us that story is everywhere, and through story we learn about the world in transformative ways.[6] Drawing on Indigenous methodologies of story, I approach this work based on the foundations of many Indigenous ancestors who utilized narrative and storytelling as a profound means to make sense of the world and our unique place in it. Indigenous scholars continue to assert the power of storytelling and narrative in not only intervening in academic spaces, but also in cultivating life for us as Indigenous peoples. Storytelling serves us by fostering a sense of collective identity, unity, and belonging, reciprocal claiming to peoples, lands, and waters, bridging the past with present with intention for the future, and locating ourselves in the vast web of relationships that make the world.[7] Story is part of the wider web of Indigenous community—an ontology *of being*.

This article is part of my story of how Diné knowledge shaped my life as a mother and human being. It is an extension of the oral history I inherited and how I make sense of it in my life as a Diné person. This is the story and knowledge I needed as a new parent, as I journeyed beside someone who lives within the intersectional spaces of Indigeneity and "disability." For years we navigated and fought against structures engrained with systemic ableism—defined by abolitionist community educator Talila Lewis as a system "of assigning value to people's bodies and minds based on societally constructed ideas of normalcy."[8] The narratives I was told about my child did not match the way I saw her, and the systems charged with her care often replicated social and political marginalization beyond what she already experienced as an Indigenous person.

She is more than what systems and diagnoses tell her she is. Diné people deserve to have their own ancestral knowledges of "disability" at the fore; to have strong kinship for all our diverse relations and to affirm their inherent belonging within our communities and institutions that serve them. This article desires to reconnect wider community back into relationship with our diverse relations and to advance the teachings that it is up to us to ensure our responsible actions work toward the care and protection of all our Diné people. This article is a call to be accountable and build on our foundations of *k'é* to combat systemic ableism and move beyond conceptualizing "disability" only within Western constructs[9] but to see "disability" as a set of teachings applicable to all of Diné people to build community that supports *all* our diverse relations.

Most importantly, this article is a small piece of a larger body of work in which I wanted to rewrite the social narrative of disability for my child. I wanted it drawn from our cultural wisdom as a gift and a promise, that our Diné ancestors loved her unconditionally. Our ancestors were meticulous in their planning for all our children who come to us in their own *ways of being.* Our ancestors placed the stories of those teachings all around us and in the natural world to remind us how to live in relationship. The focus on relational ways of knowing matters. It has always mattered.

My intervention with this work is to open space for Indigenous studies to reframe disability discourse within our own ontological frameworks. This is a first step in creating dialogue for further discussion for Indigenous peoples to begin theorizing disability on their terms and through their own epistemic orientations. It is my hope that Indigenous narratives will continue to reshape approaches to "disability" dialogue with the tenants of *belonging* over inclusion, and relationships as a fundamental condition *of being* that are not constructed, but rather inherently and persistently there to be honored.[10] With the call to engage story within disability justice discourse,[11] disability activist and scholar Alice Wong argues that the power of story moves to "show disabled people simply *being* in our own words" and on their own terms.[12] I join this discussion to examine *ontologies of being* illuminated by Diné knowledge found in stories from the land and ancestral teachings passed down from oral traditions. I *relate* these teachings to the concept of "disability" found in story and share my interpretation of them as a Diné person.

My audience for this work is intended to be Diné people and Indigenous peoples more broadly. This work is dedicated to upholding our collective archives articulated by and for us to be applied toward the theorization of "disability" rather than relying on language and theoretical constructs of disability from outside our epistemic knowledge. It is intended to contribute to the archive that is absent in the fields of disability studies and Native American studies. It aims to operate from a distinct Diné perspective with intention to speak to Diné people for our own purposes and planning. My intention for this work is to "speak forward"[13] as Cree social worker Amber Dion reminds us, "speaking the language of possibility" without an exhaustive response to engulfing structures of oppression and the subsequent entangled discourse that follows.[14] From the powerful mentorship of Indigenous women,[15] refusal to focus all my efforts on deconstructing the actions of colonizing apparatuses and structures (although vital) is to open important space for directing my words and thoughts to the people who matter most; my Diné people. This approach is a form of critical engagement through Indigenous methodologies and part of the larger movement of decolonization. To speak forward is to give life and energy to the hopeful aspiration for the future of Diné children with disabilities with an enduring point of reference to our homelands and our collective story of cascading relationships. This work lives within this space of generative world building dedicated to imagining possibilities for diverse Diné children and the futurity of all our relations.

This article first discusses my methodological approach and positionality in why I write about ancestral stories. This is followed by my retelling of the story of Early Twilight Dawn Boy. I introduce two key concepts—*hozhó* and *SNBH*—which convey the aspirations of Diné ancestral teachings that underpin the values of this story. Next, I discuss Diné methodology—that is, how those values are written onto the land through land-based knowledge found in Diné educational pedagogy. Then, I explain the lifeway of *k'é* (positive relationships)—a sophisticated way of relating and being known embedded in Diné educational pedagogy and conveyed through story. *K'é* is important to both understand the relational context of diverse *ways of being* but also the subsequent understandings of care, respect, and accountability. I conclude with some analysis of how the story of Early Twilight Dawn Boy is applied to today's issues and utilized in the fight against systemic ableism found in Diné communities and beyond.

COMING TO STORY: A DINÉ METHODOLOGY

Several years ago, I came across a story that took up disability from a Diné perspective. At the time, it was the only story I had ever heard that focused on "disability" from within my community. The primary figure in the story is a young boy. His name is Early Twilight Dawn Boy. Although he is described as someone who is disabled, the story's focus was not entirely centered on his ability or inability. In fact, the concept of "disability" in this story is not necessarily located to one definable thing or person, unlike dominant understandings of disability. From the story, the concept of "disability" is a *relative term* that signals an array of relational teachings. Many things can embody the teachings of "disability." These teachings are associated with their relational nature rather than the condition or presumed limitations of a singular person. This also is reflected in Diné language. Over the years I have heard many terms for disability without a universal term associated to this concept. As a descriptive language, each person will describe disability differently, depending on their own worldview, perspective, and style of communicating.

Relational teachings and relational understandings *of being* influence how I approach what is commonly taken for granted as being *known*. I use "disability" as a placeholder in the context of Diné perspective—my perspective. The quotation marks signal that I am speaking about what is socially understood as "disability" but that it may not equally translate to the ways in which disability is globally understood as an identity, or according to legal and medical descriptions. I believe Diné conceptualizations of "disability" are relational because Diné knowledge situates us to relate first. I have previously argued that Diné knowledge often asserts that people are known through their relational *ways of being* rather than an identity that is imposed from the outside. This is evident in the practice of *k'é*, which is invoked as a way of relating marked by how Diné establish connections between family networks in our clan system, called *k'ei*.[16] Such a relational practice grounds the ways we make ourselves known—via formal introductions— through relationship to wider community and land. When I was taught to introduce myself, I was taught to say *Shi éi Kiinya'aannii yinishyé*, I am Towering House People. Not, "I belong to the Towering House People clan," or "my clan is Towering House People." *I am Towering House People.* I am the extension of my ancestors. I come with relations that have and do exist beyond my own human knowledge. This is who I am. In our matrilineal society, this is our identity regardless of what other *ways of being* we may carry. In this way, I am a relative first. In this way, my relations are vast. *In this way, I am known through relationship.* Therefore, the way that *k'é* manifests is a relational ontology of *being*. K'é reconfigures and pushes back against dominant, imposed ways of *being known*. This complex system of *k'é*—as a powerful relational ontology—exists everywhere in the physical world and within Diné sociopolitical and spiritual life. K'é helps us unravel relational teachings of Diné educational pedagogy, which then illuminate the teachings of "disability" found in the story of Early Twilight Dawn Boy.

The story of Early Twilight Dawn Boy was shared with me in my home several years ago by the Pfeiffer family—a well-regarded family in our Diné community.[17] The story was gifted to us by the Pfeiffer family as encouragement and as something that could give us hope as I struggled at such a profound time. Instead of pointing me toward structures that had already marginalized us, they brought both myself and my child back into our community and to the teachings of care, hope, and restoration. This story changed my life and impacted how my child would come to learn about herself, immersed in Diné knowledge and love. When I informed the Pfeiffers that I was interested in sharing this story, they were supportive and said it was up to me to decide what to do with it; that I would have to determine how I would be responsible with it. With this great honor and accountability, I wanted to share aspects of the story and bring it into conversation with already published works on elements found within the story to explain how I understood the teachings of "disability."

I also heard a similar story told by Diné elder Dr. Herman Cody at the Diné Early Childhood Summit in 2021[18] and by Diné knowledge sharer Lorenzo Jim in early 2022[19] in his presentation on wellness focused on the teachings of children associated with each mountain of *Nihi Kéyah* (homelands).[20] Although similar in some ways, there are key differences in these stories. This is part of the beautiful inherent diversity of our oral traditions. The values drawn from the story remain the same, but the ways in which knowledge and concepts are circulated, cultivated, and shared depend on the person telling the story. Following suit, I retell the story of Early Twilight Dawn Boy through my own lens and style of storytelling. In doing so, I have intentionally left key things out and have tried to only share the information that I could connect back to things that have already been written about in Diné scholarship. This is part of the ethical accountability in keeping the story safe and keeping it rooted within our Diné community. Retelling this story is both a blessing and a profound responsibility. I tell this story based on my own growing knowledge of Diné teachings, and unique positionality as someone who has life experience that resonates with aspects of the story: marginalization, struggle, love, perseverance, and hope.

In retelling this story, I contend that there is no one Diné worldview. The scope of Diné stories and how they change and are interpreted illustrate this principle. Even as I retell this story, it will vary from other versions of the story, or contain different philosophical aspects. Everyone will have their own interpretation of stories and application of the teachings to their unique experience in the world. This is what Viola Cordova described as a matrix.[21] Diné scholar Lloyd Lee utilizes this approach as well, as he contends that Diné perspectives are indeed varied with different views and approaches to Diné knowledge.[22] Each perspective is unique and comes with its own set of relations and experiences to make up one's worldview. The value of these stories rests in the creativity and critical thinking used to apply them to our lives to further our understanding of ourselves, which in turn impacts the wider community. This process is reciprocal accountability—to learn about oneself in order to sustain and cultivate a community toward positive outcomes. I am more interested in the values and lessons that we take away from these teachings and how we place them within our own living experience to enact a balanced, harmonious life.

There are many more deeper meanings, sub-stories, and expansive knowledge that branches out from this story.[23] However, I keep focus on the main people in the story and the guiding principles of *k'é* (positive relationships) and prevailing values that are rooted in Diné life and ontology—the nature of existing and *being*. I do this because

I am focused on mapping the relational ways of knowing that I see as foundational to the teachings of "disability." Relational ways of knowing are both theory and method, and method has the power to direct people to know and live by the teachings of care, respect, love, and interdependence. These principles emerge as I later focus on Diné concepts of k'é, hozhó, and SNBH found in Diné educational pedagogy, which I use as a lens to engage the teachings of the story. When drawing on these powerful ontological concepts, I utilize widely published works by Diné authors and writers to engage in textual analysis in linking aspects of the story to frameworks found in our lifeways. I tried to rely on what was already written or publicly shared to avoid speaking out of place as a Diné person. My logic for telling stories and for writing about Diné knowledge, even as I am on my lifelong journey of learning what these concepts mean, stems from my foundation of k'é as the "philosophical and political anchor for my own work."[24] I do this work in the spirit of love, with hope that it helps other Diné community members and providers to understand that there is a framework for the care of all our relations and their unique ways of being.

It is vital to read this story in line with the framework of Diné epistemology. The story of Early Twilight Dawn Boy is about Diné life and the powerful relational ontologies that emerge throughout Diné thinking that embed themselves in Diné social and political worlds. This story is part of a larger history of how Diné people live their lives according to our teachings. This story comes with its own origins, lineage, relationships, lessons, and love that existed through upward of 500 years of colonialism. I share it with reverence and respect to my community, and with the hope that teachings gleaned from this story help Diné people to better understand our systems of care and responsibility to all life. In turn, I hope that it changes the lived conditions of our diverse relations and the collective movement to come together as a people, to support, care, and restore our relations to our Diné peoples with disabilities.

THE STORY OF EARLY TWILIGHT DAWN BOY

Many years ago, there was a child whose name was Early Twilight Dawn Boy. He was a thoughtful child and showed care and concern for others. He was also a person who could not walk, and in today's thinking would be considered "disabled." He lived in an area that was kept away from the village along with other children like him. Together, they existed on the margins of this community, and were excluded from all the others because people considered them as in the way. However, each day the family of Early Twilight Dawn Boy would bring food and water to the children, and each day it was Early Twilight Dawn Boy who took responsibility to share with the others.

One day, Early Twilight Dawn Boy had an idea to venture out beyond where they lived. Having never left their home, he got up one morning and waved to the other children to follow him.

Early Twilight Dawn Boy led the way and took turns helping all the others. Together they scooted along, and he tended to the others, so they all went forward together. They would go a little way, and then he would turn back to help the others who were behind come forward. He went back and forth each time, to ensure everyone stayed together and that they would move forward together.

That morning, the children went to *Ha'a'aah* (East). They were gone all day, and in the evening they returned covered in white mud. Early Twilight Dawn Boy, as he had always done, continued his commitment of care to the others even though he was very tired from the journey.

The next morning, the children went out again, but this time toward *Shádi'ááh* (South). Just like the day before, they were gone all day long. When they returned, they were covered in blue mud and their hands were caked in blue. Again, Early Twilight Dawn Boy led the way and went back and forth helping the others along as they slowly moved away from the village and then back again over the horizon. When they returned that evening, Early Twilight Dawn Boy, just as the night before, continued with his practice of care.

This continued the next day as well. However, this time toward *'E'e'aah* (West). This time upon their return, they were covered in yellow mud and their hands and bodies blended in with the setting sun and the light upon the rocks. Early Twilight Dawn Boy again, after a long journey, helped the others and did not complain about it. He carried on, just as he had always done.

At this time, it was noticed that each day the children left the community. The first couple of days had passed with little care from the others. One older man contemplated the reason for their departure each day. At first, he thought that the children were just headed out of the village to roll in the mud in the hills. "They are just making a mess," he thought to himself. "Just let them do it." And he decided not to think on it further.

However, it was on the third day that he realized they returned covered with mud in an unusual way. He became determined to follow them the next day to see what they were doing. Sure enough, as the sun rose the next day, Early Twilight Dawn Boy led the way, and as the older man had predicted, this time the children headed to *Náhookǫs* (North).

As he trailed behind, he watched Early Twilight Dawn Boy continue to lead and support the children, and he was amazed by their perseverance.

He finally came upon a valley and looked over the ledge to see the children below. They were again covered in mud, but this time it was black mud. They were playing in the light of the sun. Surrounding them were pieces of pottery they had made from the mud. They laughed and smiled at their creations, and their hands and arms were coated in black mud.

Their happiness and joy overwhelmed the man, and in that moment he realized something he had never noticed before, that they were "*healthy in all ways.*" He saw their joy and it filled the valley. Their joy was manifest in their art.

Early Twilight Dawn Boy, noticing that they had been followed, acknowledged and went toward the man. The man, who was simultaneously overcome with both happiness and sadness, walked toward Early Twilight Dawn Boy.

"What are you doing here?" said the older man.

Early Twilight Dawn Boy paused and looked out to the valley and children. He replied, "We are happy here. We are enjoying ourselves. Go back to the people and tell everyone what you saw here." The man stared in confusion as Early Twilight Dawn Boy continued, "we have been treated like a burden our whole lives. We are not coming home."

The man did not know what to say because he knew this was true.

He looked up to see the children playing in the brightest light of the warmth of the sun. They were suddenly wrapped within a sunbeam, pouring over them and lighting up the valley below. A rainbow touched the ground underneath them. In an instant, they all took flight, as birds, beautiful birds of every color and shape and they flew away into the light of the rainbow.

The man looked down, and Early Twilight Dawn Boy was gone too.

The man stood in disbelief. He was alone in the valley with the pottery that lined the grass where the children had played. He tried to think about what he had just seen when he was overcome with grief. He realized the loss of his relatives, and when he returned to the people they were remorseful in their actions.

According to Chad Pfeiffer, in this way the teachings of Early Twilight Dawn Boy speak to us to this day. They remind us of the accountability embedded in relationships and the rules of *k'é* that organize our responsibility to all life and people.

They speak to the accountability of care and compassion,
to live in the spirit of love, and kinship with one another.
They also point to the ways that Early Twilight Dawn Boy
becomes the point of reference, in achieving the unbelievable. He is the one who illustrates that he is always there
to help. He demonstrated leadership and the embodiment
of *k'é* and teachings of compassion, care and the principles

of enjoying life. He was spiritually blessed to lead the path of others and pursue the life of being healthy in all ways.[25]

SNBH AND WAYS OF BEING:
KNOWING THROUGH STORY

There is an entire worldview and philosophy of Diné ontology encapsulated in the story of Early Twilight Dawn Boy. Although this is a story about a young boy and children, the focus of who they were was not entirely situated on a notion of ability or inability. Early Twilight Dawn Boy was equally described as a leader, caretaker, and artist. More importantly, he was a teacher as his life and story embodied the Diné pursuit and lifeway of *Sa ąh Naaghái Bik'eh Hózhóón*,[26] commonly referred to as *SNBH*. The focus of the teachings of "disability" rests within the value system encased in this profound lifeway, which is the focus of this section. Shifting briefly to a discussion of SNBH and its manifestation in teachings found in Diné educational pedagogy is needed to unravel the scope of relational ontologies found within the story and to understand the values which underpin them.

As a "vital foundational paradigm in Diné thought,"[27] *SNBH* is a sacred term and Diné scholars insist that it cannot be reduced to individual meanings of the words.[28] Entire books and dissertations have been written about what this concept means,[29] and many Diné scholars argue that there is not a comprehensive, definitive answer.[30] Rather, it is easier to explain how *SNBH* manifests in one's life journey rather than to try to explain what it is exactly.[31] Due to the complexity of its meaning and how it expresses itself differently in everyone's life, narrative and storytelling are treasured conduits for the exploration of *SNBH*.[32] Story draws out meaning of what this foundational principle is rather than attempting to lodge this concept as definable, concrete thing. Therefore, *SNBH* also informed my reasoning to refuse to define "disability" within a Diné context as a concrete, definable thing. Again, the relational nature of both these concepts are unraveled through story and intellectual pedagogy becomes the tool to understand them.

Insight from Diné scholars helps give shape to a conceptual frame for this lifeway without confining it. According to Diné scholars, *SNBH* is the aspiration that underwrites all Diné teachings. Diné scholar Vincent Werito describes *SNBH* as "who we are . . . what we strive for, what we hope for and pray for because we believe that its essence and meaning lie at the base of our language and cultural identity and traditional cultural knowledge and teachings."[33] Similarly, Diné leader and scholar Rex Lee Jim offers a basic conceptual understanding of *SNBH* as "the beauty in life realized through application of teachings that work."[34] Diné scholar Lloyd Lee also frames *SNBH* as a process that is encased in aspirations, values, and teachings of Diné knowledge in which *SNBH* is the expression of a life journey that is complete and balanced.[35] However, *SNBH* is not merely an abstract concept. *SNBH* is central to Diné ceremonial knowledge and is the basis for Diné educational pedagogy,[36] a relational way of knowing found within Diné land-based knowledge that encases the values Diné hold dear.

The story of Early Twilight Dawn Boy illustrates how his life was the medium for teaching a set of values'and principles intended to help people understand the concept of *SNBH*. The teachings of "disability" are therefore committed to relational ways of knowing, relating, and caretaking rooted in aspirations oriented toward *SNBH*. The focus was how the people in the story lived their lives, and how they engaged in the world of relationships. The story was also about imbalanced relationships, and how reciprocal accountability operates as a mechanism for restoration and a life of *SNBH*. It requires an interaction of relationships—from relationships with one's inner self to one's land and community. This understanding of wider relations make the world within Diné ontology. According to Lee, "SNBH also guides a person and the community to completeness, whereby balance and harmony are the norm and not the exception."[37] The story of Early Twilight Dawn Boy helps Diné understand what this idea of completeness is when we look at the teachings of story and the wider relations in which they take place, from the deep spaces of our internal worlds as they extend outward to the natural world. All of these relations make certain conditions that either build and sustain, or that create conditions of imbalance and harm.

One way to try to further understand *SNBH* comes from Werito's focus on the relational concept from the phrase *SNBH*: *hózhó*.[38] Although Werito contends that this word *hózhó* also lacks a concrete definition, he links this term to the aspirations for "harmonious outcomes"[39] or living in a harmonious "way that is in line with the life force of nature."[40] *Hozhó* can be understood through its relational essence as well, particularly as it relates to story. This concept is grounded in *Hózhóójí* (Blessing Way) teachings, which are an integral part of Diné lifeway.[41] Throughout different stories, particularly Diné Blessing Way stories, the concepts of *SNBH* and *hózhó* are embedded in numerous representations found in the natural world, all of which operate like a "compass."[42] Blessing Way stories are stories that teach morals and values necessary to guide and direct people toward a harmonious life.[43] According to Diné poets Rex Lee Jim and Mitchell Blackhorse, the utility of story is to "make one think, to reflect, and that such a reflection should motivate one to proper behaviour."[44] Stories not only teach the individual, but also cultivate the community toward a collective movement of *hozhó*. Diné educator Kevin Belin argues that teachings are intended to "create boundaries, teach responsibilities and how it *to care for one another*, about how to build trust and guard that trust . . . through responsibility and helping one another."[45] The relational lessons within these stories connect people to themselves, to their community, and to the wider world. The goal is to strive for harmonious outcomes through these many connections.

These aspirations emerge through story and rest within the concepts of *SNBH* that have orientation to land. This framework that encompasses the natural world is often referred to as the Sun Wise Path Teachings according to Werito[46] or "A Journey of Wellness . . . by the Journey of the Sun" by Diné educator Manley Begay.[47] Both of these frameworks contain the values and principles that lead one toward an understanding of what *SNBH* and *hózhó* are. This framework is also reflected in Diné educational pedagogy because it represents a physical, tangible system of relationship based in the natural world and *Nihi Kéyah* (homelands). To come to know these concepts is to come to know them through relationships, learning, living, and reflecting. To learn them is *to be* in the world. Ultimately, this unravels the purpose of this framework, which Werito argues "guide[s] how an individual lives and develops respect and/or reverence for self, his or her relatives and the natural world."[48] Ancestral stories are both theorizations and methods of how to live a life of completeness—how to live in a *hózhó* way and pursue *SNBH* toward completeness.

Stories have concrete lessons, but also have more abstract, philosophical knowledge woven in them that pertains to these vast relations in the world. These different representations in relation to the concepts of *hózhó* and *SNBH* have material connections that are rooted in the natural world. This "compass"[49] does not operate in a linear way but is multilayered and dimensional. It has order and that order is understood through land and through life processes. The culmination of these various layers can be understood as the framework of Diné educational pedagogy. Diné educator Alberta Curley describes this system as an "organizational chart" that interconnects countless teachings to the immediate contexts of Diné individual and community life.[50] Diné educational pedagogy is fundamentally land-based knowledge that operates within an intricate web of relationships that aids in helping a person understand these lifeways of *SNBH* and *hózhó*—to learn of oneself, be creative, overcome life's challenges, and understand our expansive relationships with the foundations of Diné values attached to them. These in turn cultivate a sense of belonging, which Werito contends points us to find "hope, faith, respect and reverence for life."[51] Immersion in these values as they surround Diné people in the physical world teaches Diné people by connecting them and demonstrating how to relate so that we might collectively inherit the blessings of these teachings.

Therefore, Diné stories and principles are inscribed into our lands, and into the traditional territories of Diné people.[52] Diné education is about our identity as Diné people, and our identity is predicated on relationships and relational understandings of *being* in the world. Diné education is a lifelong process that is fundamentally rooted in relationships and is oriented toward living a life in balance, *hózhó* and *SNBH*. Diné educational pedagogy situates Diné people in a constant place of learning through living, and through land-based pedagogy where engagement with our connections in the world around us become the medium for learning. I argue that this relational way of knowing is the framework in which teachings of "disability" emerge from the story of Early Twilight Dawn Boy. The following section explores the teachings of land that are referenced within this important story. These teachings embedded in the land all are oriented within the aspirations and values of *hozhó* and *SNBH*.

DINÉ EDUCATIONAL PEDAGOGY

Diné teachings are encapsulated in *Nihi Kéyah* (homelands), sometimes called *Dinétah* according to older oral traditions.[53] They are marked by four sacred mountains that create our ancestral boundaries that we are born and given to as Diné people.[54] There are teachings for countless places, directions, and stories of these places.[55] Teachings are also embedded in tangible items, such as tools, rocks, and plants. These teachings portrayed through these elements, items, and places manifest in stories about people, particularly important figures in our creation narratives.[56] Teachings always include reference to the four cardinal directions and sacred mountains found in each of those directions. This is significant because Diné epistemology is made known through land. This orientation gives reference and shape to Diné knowledge.

This framework is the basis for Diné educational pedagogy. These teachings surround people in their everyday lives through this land-based system.[57] Implanting lessons in the natural world not only gives orientation to one's place, but also a site of nurturing where we inherently belong and grow.[58] In this way, Diné are born and will *always* have a place, a sense of belonging, and a framework that treasures our inherent inclusion. *SNBH* and the possibility of *hózhó*, as a state of being, learning, and doing, are available to Diné people, and it is modeled for us through story and land-based knowledge.

Ancestral teachings were made to reflect the world around us and could be found anywhere in Diné life. An important feature of Diné pedagogy is that it weaves worlds together through the constant practice of rooting relationships in all things and situating critical thinking and self-realization into a process of interrelatedness mirrored in the physical world.[59] Bridging the contexts of oneself to the wider world establishes an understanding of relationality and interdependence. Werito contends that "the principles of *hózhó* as they exist in Diné thought are inherently a form of critical thinking" in a lifelong process of "naming the world, actions and reflection that results in transformation."[60] The approach to learning through this pedagogy relies on understanding the world through the lens of relationship and making those connections between numerous things and through the many aspects of our lived experience. According to Diné poet Jake Skeets, this model encapsulates Diné thought and "sets the Diné universe," with *SNBH* as a layered philosophy that is "the embodiment of living through all things."[61] We are connected to an intricate constellation of relational ontologies. These ontologies are interwoven in the natural world.

Although *SNBH* is intangible, it is integral to the four cardinal directions: *Ha'a'aah* (East), *Shádi'ááh* (South), *'E'e'aah* (West), and *Náhookǫs* (North).[62] It is connected to the four scared mountains that create the boundary of *Dinétah*, the lands that Diné were born from and to.[63] Those mountains are *Sis Naajiní, Tsoodził, Dook'o'oosłííd*, and *Dibé Nitsaa*.[64] According to Diné elder Wilson Aronilth Jr., *SNBH* is connected to the four phases of the day: early twilight dawn, blue twilight, yellow evening twilight, and folding darkness.[65] It also connected to phases of human life: infancy, childhood, adulthood, and old age.[66] It embodies stages of growth and learning: thoughts/critical thinking represented to the East, planning to the South, reasoning through application in life to the West, and creativity, assurance, reflection to the North.[67]

It is also tied to inner development of the person: the mental, physical, emotional, and spiritual dimensions that make a person

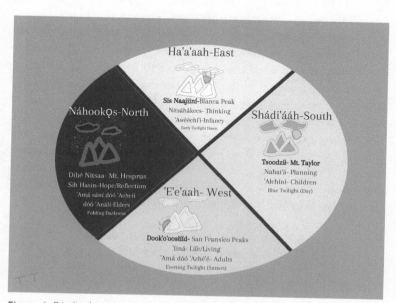

Figure 1. Diné relational teachings model (Color is part of the model. White represents East, Blue/Turquoise represents South, Yellow represents West, and Black represents North), Tifa Rain, 2022.

whole.[68] All these dimensions are considered vital in thinking of the wellness of a person throughout their life and contributes to the sense of completeness conceptualized through *SNBH*. Both an individual day and lifetime are reflected in this model. The process of making connections and understanding the relational *ways of being* through various dimensions matter when conceptualizing what it means to be complete.

This is the most basic framework of Diné teachings and is reflected in the chart in Figure 1.[69] There are more layers that are embedded in countless other cultural practices and things: for example, the *hoghaan* (home/house)[70] and the lifeway of weaving.[71] However, the main point I wish to make is *that the things entwined through SNBH uphold a value system and presents a visual, personal, and spiritual compass to understand the aspects of a human being in relationship to the world.*

This system was lived and journeyed by the children in the story of Early Twilight Dawn Boy. They modeled their engagement within this system, and their journey is the embodiment of living the principles encapsulated within this complex paradigm. The children were the point of reference for knowing the interconnections and dimensions of life that led to completeness, wholeness, and self-understanding—they led to an understanding of *hózhó* and *SNBH*. The children modeled these dimensions of Diné lifeways, to live in relationship and create wholeness in synchronizing all parts of their life.[72] They demonstrated that Diné life and philosophical thinking are predicated on interrelationships and the numerous connections people experience in the world through their physical (material, tangible), spiritual (feelings, heart knowledge, connection), ancestral (memory, land, art), cultural (ceremony, philosophy, language), and mental (critical thinking, relational knowledge, perceptions, compassion) selves. This wholeness in conceptualizing the *world in relation* to oneself and vice versa, is an important methodological feature of Diné pedagogy. It is a sacred *way of being*—an ontology of *being*. Early Twilight Dawn Boy and the children were exemplars of how to live in beauty—of how to pursue SNBH. They exercised belief in themselves, lived in relationship, and built community where they were free to be who they truly are. The lessons drawn from their lives, read in tandem with Diné educational pedagogy, demonstrate how to live a life of balance, harmony, peace, and reciprocity. They teach us to live in aspiration of *SNBH*.[73]

RELATIONAL TEACHINGS OF "DISABILITY"

I now turn to examine relationality focused on physical references within the story and map them onto the wider scope of Diné intellectual pedagogy oriented toward SNBH found within the paradigm I introduced in the last section. I use the terms *reference* and *orientation* instead of the term *symbolism* to describe the things, places, directions, and phenomena in this story. Diné references in relation to aspects of our educational pedagogy are not merely metaphorical. These references to actual mountains and directions, sunbeams, and color are treated as significant relations that are integral to Diné teachings and making sense of who Diné are in the world. These references are teachers of complex knowledge systems that *are the way of the world* for Diné people. They are treated as true representations and expressions of the teachings they are connected to. They have meaning through relationship with Diné people, land, and life. When we honor that, we begin to understand them for what they are—something beyond, and more powerful than merely metaphors and symbols.

The clearest way to understand this process of relationality within the story could be to consider the question of who the story is about. Although the story is situated around one person—Early Twilight Dawn Boy—the story is about multiple things and people. The story is about lifeways that are rooted in connections. These connections are part of the wider understanding of *hózhó* and how to live well and in completeness. The story of Early Twilight Dawn Boy is a story of relationality that has many parts to it: community, land, nature, actions, emotions, perceptions, leadership, compassion, natural phenomena and elements, the sacred, and spiritual dimensions *of being* of not only people, but also of the nonhuman world. Therefore, in the story of Early Twilight Dawn Boy, the concept of "disability" is not relegated to solely one person and their attributes. Many things can embody the teachings of "disability," and the teachings associated with those things (mountains, directions, phenomena) can be found in the natural world and in everyday experience.

These physical references found in Diné pedagogy—the four directions, colors, natural elements and so forth—are part of the wider expressions of *SNBH*—a life journey that Lee discusses as sometimes called the "Corn Pollen Path," or "SNBH Trail."[74] As I previously discussed, the references in stories operate as a "compass"[75] to guide individuals to a greater understanding of relational teachings, which Werito explains link the "mind, body and spirit."[76] Similarly, Werito demonstrates this process with his four-part approach in describing *hózhó*. The first is *thinking* associated with the East, to "understand we are a piece of a greater whole."[77] The second is planning and internationalization of our thoughts to the South, "to realize who we are and what our values are."[78] The third is action through living to the West, "in advocating for self and others."[79] Finally, refection through "having hope, faith, respect and reverence for life" to the North.[80] This four-part framework of our Diné lifeway paradigm is encased in numerous teachings that are interrelated and function toward individual wholeness and community well-being. They are taught to Diné people through the teachings encased in the natural world.

When the various teachings within this vast system of Diné ontology are placed together, we see how various dimensions of Diné thinking link together a broad scope of how Diné thought teaches us to see *the bigger picture* of our world, and how we are endlessly connected to it. Each teaching can be very distinct but is made *known* through a series of relational processes that cascade into even more teachings and lessons that lead to continual processes of growth. Diné educator Kevin Belin calls this cyclic form of knowledge as "stories within stories," which are in a state of constant expanse and growth.[81] This is the power of Diné teachings to continually build on and cultivate in multidirectional and multilayered ways.

Focusing on constellations of relationality, the story of Early Twilight Dawn Boy introduces ontologies *of being* that consider nonhuman relationships. When this story was shared with me, Pfeiffer told me that whenever I saw a rainbow, or birds, I would be reminded about the story.[82] That it would be with me wherever I went. I realized that the use of reference placed the concept of "disability" everywhere. The teachings were embedded in nature and in the everyday moments of my life. "Disability" as a concept was not reduced to a specific *way of being* that was predicated on sole aspects of ability relevant to only one person. "Disability" was a multilayered concept that placed a value system of relational teachings into the world that impacted everyone. "Disability" is not an isolated thing or condition. In Diné ontology, these connections functioned in situating the order and importance of these beliefs as central to community life and living. They were placed into the community and into the natural world. Through reference and land, through relationality, the values associated with these references were grounded everywhere in Diné life.

The stories are both represented and manifest in the natural world, where objects, natural occurrences, plants, animals, and places become the carriers of the story. By articulating the complex web of interconnections as pedagogy for understanding the lifeway of *SNBH* and *hózhó*, the vast scope of interconnections become evident everywhere we go, in everything we experience. There is power in placing stories in the natural world, whereby our existence and relationships become a pedagogy and medium for learning how to live the concepts of Diné ontology. That is why *SNBH* is often explained through story and narrative of actual experience of living in the world. Affirming Werito's commitment to not define these concepts of *SNBH* and *hózhó*, he maintains that "hózhó is more significant when the meaning is conceptualized, actualized, lived and reflected on in a person level."[83] I see this approach as something that can theoretically apply to the concept of "disability" as well.

The teachings of "disability" as a conceptual framework are everywhere in the world. It is through relationships that I understand how these teachings are applied to my life and wider community. Placement in the world through material reference and orientation makes this pedagogy and its teachings available to everyone. They are constant reminders of the lessons tied to this story; the teachings associated with "disability" are everywhere. From the story of Early Twilight Dawn Boy, I realize that many things embody the concept and teachings of "disability," and through the teachings we realize we all have relationship, and therefore accountability to all life and people.

As a relational framework, the completeness of one's life impacts the wholeness of a community.[84] This is why Diné scholar Lloyd Lee contends that to know SNBH and the harmonious outcomes of hózhó depends on relational understandings of community.[85] Across many Indigenous nations, there is a common thread of worldview that establishes that there is no separation between a person and the world we live in.[86] The individual is always understood in relation to the community. There is autonomy, but it differs from constructed definitions of "independence" of settler society. Both Māori advocate Johnathan Tautari and Tewa scholar Gregory Cajete argue that autonomy provides for an individual's unique way of thinking, planning, and acting predicated on their preferences and individual self-aspirations.[87] However, the individual is still seen as themselves but in relationship to others. This is what upholds the basis for reciprocal accountability that demands responsibility for oneself, but also responsibility to our communities. Such a reciprocal process still honors the unique *ways of being* and choices of individuals but frames them in the context of the wider community.[88] This moves the concept of "disability" away from the individualistic perspective so prevalent in wider sociopolitical discourse and rather shifts towards a community perspective that is rooted in relationships and the inherent rubrics of care and reciprocal accountability.

The relationships that we constantly live in and through must be acknowledged and cared for. It is not only because of the reciprocal nature of necessity for practical survival, but because Diné practices of relating are part of how Diné make sense of the world. Therefore, Diné teachings embedded in story direct us to know ourselves through relationship.[89] Diné educational pedagogy reconfigures a way to *know* of diverse *ways of being* through a web of infinite connections. These connections are cradled within the heart of *hozhó* and are rooted in aspirations of completeness through SNBH. They uphold the promise of belonging, and the intention of cultivating harmonious outcomes for *all* people.

Instilling and Nurturing Positive Relationships: *K'é*

A foundational aspect of relational ways of knowing can be also be unpacked through the Diné lifeway of *k'é*, which I choose to describe as positive relationships. According to Diné scholar Lloyd Lee, *k'é* "reinforces respect, kindness, cooperation, friendliness, reciprocity and love."[90] It is "positive" because I understand it in line with the aspiration and intention of *hozhó*—harmonious outcomes that stem from our beautiful actions in the world and the knowledge applied to how we live. However, there are lessons about the absence of *k'é* and examples of what happens when we live without this foundational way of relating. Hardship, marginalization, unbalanced or absent relations, stigma, and neglect are all facets of the absence of *k'é*. These were demonstrated within the story of Early Twilight Dawn Boy and can be recognized in today's conditions in which diverse Diné children and their family live.

The story of Early Twilight Dawn Boy within a relational scope conveys how many things inform our understanding of "disability." Teachings of "disability" in this story are foregrounded by relationality, which links back to the principles of *k'é* (positive relationships), love, and accountability. This compels individuals to consider their own relationship to the teachings of "disability," even if they themselves are not directly impacted by it. Teachings of "disability" through relationality have lessons for all Diné people and the story of Early Twilight Dawn Boy demonstrates this by placing it within the expression and framework of *SNBH* and *hózhó* as fundamentality rooted in countless systems of relationship and as a life process.

K'é as a lifeway is a principle of how to relate and be accountable in sustaining *SNBH*, love, and unity with all our relations. *K'é* is about relating in multidimensional ways while holding dear the principles of *hózhó* toward *SNBH*, resulting in the desire for balance and responsibility through relationships. *K'é*, from my own understanding and journey toward *SNBH*, teaches me to live in relationship and through connection with others and the world around me. Through that relationship, I am blessed with not only a place (belonging), but also accountability (relations). I am compelled to not only aspire to live well and in balance, but also with the intention to contribute for others to live well and in balance, through reciprocity; to respect and honor the balance and inherent rights of others as they pursue *SNBH* in their own lives through their own relations and processes. This is the fruit and the treasures of living in relationship. Failure to understand and honor all these dimensions leads to imbalance.[91]

Imbalance is hardship, isolation, marginalization, and all things that manifest when others do not respect themselves, others, or the natural world.[92] Imbalance is another definition of systemic ableism, in which people do not honor nor support the unique *ways of being* of all our relations, the inherent diversity within the world, and our collective responsibility to caretake all life and people. Therefore, the importance of *k'é* (positive relationships) foregrounds a balanced pursuit of living, well-being, nurturing, and thriving of Diné land and life through our own cultural contexts. These teachings also speak to the ways in which harm and imbalance present themselves when we fail to honor all these dimensions of living. According to Diné language experts Evangeline Parsons-Yazzie and Margaret Speas, "the traditional teachings about k'é show the Navajo people how to maintain self-control and social control" to caretake our communities toward proper living and care.[93] Stories are examples of how to uphold our accountability to the multi-relations we have: to people, the natural world, our inner selves, our actions, and our lifelong journey through our distinct practices of k'é. Relations are a profound part of ontology—what it means to be and exist in the world. The story of Early Twilight Dawn Boy opens space for these value systems to perpetuate, and for people to locate themselves within a system to relationship. Such a shift places the individual in direct relation with the teachings of "disability," which I view are teachings of k'é and SNBH. In this, there is a call for Diné people to pursue these teachings toward community wholeness and caretaking our diverse relations.

WHERE THE PATHWAY CAN LEAD US

From the story of Early Twilight Dawn Boy, I argued that the questions of ability are not framed solely around the physical and cognitive aspects of a person. *Rather, they are more concerned with the relational framework of SNBH and how it is upheld.* I believe the teachings convey the power of entrenched values in different aspects of Diné educational pedagogy. The first is the relational self—thinking for oneself and following one's heart. Early Twilight Dawn Boy did this. He did not accept the wider beliefs about who he was or how things should be. He nurtured himself by taking his thoughts and believing in himself, his own self-determination and sovereignty. This led to the second part of *knowing* himself. He internalized his right to pursue his strengths and creative nature, and to live in relationships. Because of this, he could recognize these gifts in others. His journey impacted this smaller community of the children in profound ways on their own journeys. The third part was his actualization of these beliefs into his planning and actions to do what he believed and to advocate for others. He built community on the principles of care, respect, and love. Finally, he came to a place where the fruits of his journey to find hope, respect, and acceptance of himself was complete and he shared it with the other children. In doing so, I believe that their flight into the rainbow was the signal of the epitome of these teachings. To me, their flight conveyed they lived in completeness, in relationship, in *SNBH, and in sovereignty* as they left in the light of the rainbow. Their responsible actions brought beauty into the world. Their lives are the model and point of reference for living *hózhó* and the teachings of *SNBH*, to follow the Corn Pollen Path.

I have outlined how *SNBH* is a guide to orient Diné lives toward aspirations of wellness, love, self-understanding, and relationship to the various world(s) we live in. Wilson Aronilth Jr. reminds us that *SNBH* directs individuals to become empowered in who they are.[94] *SNBH* honors collective cultivation through acknowledgment of inherent diversity in the world and importance of individual life journeys and *ways of being*. *SNBH* compels people to be self-reflective of their own actions and thoughts, and how they relate to the world around them.[95] Such a practice is reciprocal accountability; to be accountable for ourselves, our thoughts, and actions, but to also be accountable to those around us. As a community practice, uniting our aspirations to move toward the teachings of *SNBH* within reciprocal accountability benefits us all.[96]

From my engagement with the story, I come to understand that teachings of "disability" are teachings of *hózhó*, which teach us how to live a harmonious and balanced life of completeness, and wellness on my own journey on the Corn Pollen Path. "Disability" and *SNBH* are therefore deeply related. Early Twilight Dawn Boy's life and story are the point of reference *of being* in a sacred way. His story is about teaching others how to live in a sacred way and pursue *SNBH*. "Disability," therefore, is not compartmentalized as something that is not personal for everyone. It is deeply personal, because it teaches us something about ourselves and aides us in our understanding of what *SNBH* is and how to pursue it. It gives us a clearer understanding of completeness predicated on relational ways of knowing embodied through the lifeway of *k'é* in grounding relationships and accountability to those relationships.

It is through those relational frameworks that the teachings of "disability" are made known. Everyone can learn about "disability" and how it relates to them and their treatment of others through the lessons in the story of Early Twilight Dawn Boy. The story upheld the journey toward *SNBH* for not only the children but for the community as well. Werito describes this as a dialectal feature in that our lives carry "potential for a harmonious (*hózhóójí*) or destructive (*naayee'íí*) path, depending on which path (or way) one seeks."[97] This story shows the possibility of both paths. This was a profound teaching moment for the community, to learn something about how their responsible actions would either bring beauty into the world or hinder others. The story offers the potential for restoration in healing from our actions and negative perceptions. It gives us hope, that people can change as a society, and that through *k'é* there is way to achieve that.

To honor *k'é* (positive relationships) is to follow the Corn Pollen Path. After all, the collective aspiration of our teachings is to pursue *SNBH*, an aspirational life process of *hózhó*—harmonious outcomes, balance, and completeness. Therefore, the teachings of how to live in beauty with cultivating belonging, love, and acknowledgment of all our diverse relations are at the core of our beliefs, and indeed are deeply reflected in this story. *K'é* brings into question the ways in which Diné philosophy teaches Diné people to understand identity as relational networks that not only strengthen belonging, empowerment, and self-worth but also provide a mechanism for accountability necessary in our communities. *K'é* is a powerful theoretical tool to undo the negative harms attached to the identity formation of "disability" within Western constructs.[98] *K'é* is a powerful tool to confront systemic ableism across *Diné Bikéyah*.

From my own understanding of this story, I argue, Diné people can never live the principles of *hózhó* if we do not account for all our Diné relatives with "disabilities." The lifelong journey to live the principles of *hózhó* and *SNBH* dictate that Diné live in relationship and accountability to all our relations. This is a model for true inclusive practices and justice that is not framed through policy or law. Rather, it is both framed and alive through relationship and inherent belonging based on Diné understandings of community and wider relations. This argument is compelled by the questions: how are Diné communities enacting and cultivating themselves toward *SNBH* with consideration to all their relations? How do *SNBH* and *hózhó*—the pursuit of harmonious outcomes—foster and resolve the fundamental desire for belonging of some of our most marginalized and stigmatized relatives? According to Lee,

> The passion to live and the desire to achieve the goals set forth by a person and the community are interwoven in SNBH . . . The Diyin Dine'é instructed the people to follow the SNBH path to ensure wellness, happiness, quality of life and sustainability. This path helps the people *believe in themselves* and have *trust in what they are doing*.[99]

The rights to live in balance and peace, with faith in oneself and trust in what we are doing, with affirmation that we belong, and are valued is part of the collective movement of *SNBH*, which is multidirectional, circular, and all inclusive. The question then becomes, how are those rights cultivated through reciprocity and accountability from our communities, educational apparatuses, and policies that engage diverse learners?

This is the place where Diné teachings make profound interventions into our structures. Notions of "inclusion" should not be a power dynamic in which we decide when and under what conditions someone can belong. Rather, we start from the place of knowing that all children inherently belong. They have a series of relationships that they are born with that extend beyond our knowledge of them. Those relationships dictate that they inherently have a place, connections, and the right to reciprocal accountability found in the teachings of *SNBH* and *k'é*. The focus then turns to us as community members, educators, and planners. It is up to us to honor those inherent gifts and relationships our learners come to us with. It is up to us to uphold those relationships as the grounds for combating systemic ableism on all fronts and recognize that we are *accountable through relationship, no matter what.*

Diné people have their own laws, customs, and practices to caretake their own relatives with "disabilities." Grounding this stance propels the need for Diné practices of *k'é* to foreground any educational planning or legal framework for our diverse members of our community. We have the systems to safeguard the protection of all our children. Those systems not only provide for inclusion and care of our most marginalized populations. They provide for the cultivation and cyclic process of well-being to emerge and flow throughout our communities and lands.

Finally, in the context of broader movements for disability justice, I view *k'é* as a Diné orientation to dismantle systemic ableism[100] in calling on all people to examine the extent of their core beliefs regarding peoples with disabilities. The intervention of rethinking disability through the lens of relationship—through *k'é, hozhó, SNBH,* and their manifestation in Diné educational pedagogy, recenters the point of focus to our own individual perceptions, biases, treatment, and beliefs about others. This Diné orientation can be used to confront the chasms that underwrite the mistreatment, marginalization, and systemic ableism that peoples with disabilities encounter through countless areas of their lives. However, looking at *k'é* as a distinct form of Diné lifeway not only gives us a modality of how to self-reflect and critique our own views, *it also produces a generative point of departure to move forward in relationship.* Therefore, a symbiotic practice of accountability emerges from relationship.

Both the children and *k'é* found within the story illustrate how perception of "disability" must be understood through relationship, which subsequently grounds the principles of reciprocal accountability. This is beyond the notion of accountability as a slew of checkmarks and ethical considerations. As educators, we must move beyond the stagnate, dehumanizing way of knowing and thinking about "disability" often written in policy[101] or through economic models within the rubrics of ability, productivity, and success.[102] We must combat the ever-growing reliance on biomedical modalities and practices of assessment—as the basis *of knowing* embedded within our educational apparatuses and processes. To know and realize our children through the system of relationships that are life-sustaining and enriching is to refocus on how to conceptualize "disability" through ways that underscore caretaking and belonging as fundamental conditions *of being*. This way of living produces a framework of reciprocal accountability that not only caretakes and honors the most marginalized in our society, but also cultivates our communities toward collective wellness and wholeness.

Well-being is multifaceted and has reciprocal qualities. As Cajete continually reminds us throughout his works as an Indigenous educator, nothing in the world exists in isolation.[103] Everything already has a relationship. Cree scholar Amber Dion has grounded this principle in saying that "we only know what we know through relationship."[104] When we establish our own well-being, it impacts others, just as if they consider our well-being, it impacts them. It is a reciprocal process. Harm is also a reciprocal process. This is why toxic ideologies and relationships that are grounded in harm, such as the disavowal or marginalization of certain individuals as seen in the story of Early Twilight Dawn Boy, demonstrate how harm is reciprocated both ways. This can change. It requires that society, and how we as people approach relationships in the multi-spheres of our lives, fundamentally change.

Diné perspectives shift the focus of "disability" to bring back into focus that it is up to all of us to ensure our responsible actions will bring beauty into the world and sustain others. It is up to us to be accountable and build more just relations with our peoples with disabilities. From the teachings of Early Twilight Dawn Boy, we become the students to learn and listen to our relatives of all diverse ways of being as they reveal to us what it means to be in beauty. That we honor their relationships, *ways of being*, and their inherent agency and sovereignty. That we learn from them in their vast *ways of being* and relating. The refocusing of a Diné lens of "disability" casts us into the webs of relationships, beyond the human and nonhuman construction, to realize that in beauty and completeness there is always a place, a journey, and a path.

AUTHOR BIOGRAPHY

Sandra Yellowhorse is Kinyaa'áani (Towering House People) born for the French of the Diné Nation. She is a PhD candidate at Te Puna Wānanga, School of Māori and Indigenous Education at Waipapa Taumata Rau, the University of Auckland. She is a mother and student of a Kinyaa'áani person who is the heart of her academic work, and also her life's joy.

ACKNOWLEDGMENTS

I extend my thanks to Tifa Rain for her creative spirit and generous heart. I love you and am blessed to be your mother. Thank you shí yázhí, for creating the Relational Teachings Model with generous consultation from Warlance Chee with the *Saad K'idilye* Diné Language Nest. Profound thanks to the Pfeiffer family for sharing this story when we needed it the most. To my Diné teachers and colleagues Dr. Lloyd

Lee and Chad Pfeiffer, and to mana wāhine Dr. Te Kawehau Hoskins and Dr. Melinda Webber, ahéhee' for your help and guidance on this work. To all the children who live like Early Twilight Dawn Boy, your gifts are abundant and teach me to live in beauty. Thank you for nurturing me in all ways.

NOTES

1 Jill Bevan-Brown, "Introduction," in *Working with Māori Children with Special Education Needs: He mahi whakahirahira* (NZCER Press, 2015), 20.

2 The social model of disability identifies disability as a "consequence" of environments and societal factors that are disabling. See Huhana Hickey, "Tātau tātau: Engaging with whanau hauā from within a Cultural Framework," in *Working with Māori Children with Special Education Needs: He mahi whakahirahira* (NZCER Press, 2015), 70–84.

3 See Vincent Werito, "Understanding Hózhó to Achieve Critical Consciousness: A Contemporary Diné Interpretation of the Philosophical Principles of Hózhó," in *Diné Perspectives: Revitalizing and Reclaiming Navajo Thought* (Tucson: University of Arizona Press, 2014).

4 Jill Bevan-Brown, "Introduction," in *Working with Māori Children with Special Education Needs: He mahi whakahirahira* (NZCER Press, 2015), 20.

5 Huhana Hickey, "Tātau tātau: Engaging with whanau hauā from within a Cultural Framework," in *Working with Māori Children with Special Education Needs: He mahi whakahirahira* (NZCER Press, 2015), 70.

6 Avery Denny, "Exploring the Diné Map of the Stars: Navajo Astronomy 101; #Be Powerful Diné Culture Camp," Iina Bihoo'aah, Facebook Live, January 27, 2022, *https://www .facebook.com/iinabihooaah*

/videos/931843267722431; and Kevin Belin, "Journey of the Hero Twins to Their Father," NACA Storyteller Series, webinar, Albuquerque, NM, February 5, 2021.

7 The importance of storytelling across Indigenous nations is addressed by numerous Indigenous scholars. See Kevin Belin, "Indigenous Art Self Care," Diné Early Childhood Summit: Practice and Teachings, webinar, August 26, 2021; Joann Archibald, Jason De Santolo, and Jenny Lee-Morgan, *Decolonizing Research: Storywork as Indigenous Methodology* (London: Zed Books, 2019); Gregory Cajete, *Indigenous Community: Rekindling the Teachings of the Seventh Fire* (Minneapolis: Living Justice Press, 2015); Linda Tuhiwai Smith, *Decolonizing Methodologies*, 2nd ed. (London: Zed Books, 2012).

8 Talila Lewis, "Working Definition of Systemic Ableism," blog, January 1, 2022, https://www .talilalewis.com/blog.

9 For more information on Western models of disability, see Huhana Hickey, "Tātau tātau: Engaging with whanau hauā from within a Cultural Framework," in *Working with Māori Children with Special Education Needs: He mahi whakahirahira* (NZCER Press, 2015), 72–73.

10 I theorize the notion of "inclusion" in mainstream disability discourse and challenge it by using Moroni Benally's reflections on the late Herbert Benally's work, that relations in Diné thought are not something that are constructed, but something that already exists. See Moroni

Benally, "For Some Time I Have Struggled with the Meaning of Relationality in Indigenous (i.e. Diné) Perspectives," Facebook, November 19, 2021, *https://www.facebook.com/moroni.benally/posts/pfbid02XosM7svvTsugELcRnpy6QgWm7mwLKMiAma7JADFTztfAiFwjVv8pcK3PtskGsHBMl.*

11 Critical disability scholars are utilizing narrative and storytelling as methods to theorize lived realities of peoples within the worlds of disability. I incorporate this call to include Diné story of lived experience to build the emergent field of Indigenous disability studies. This work is also part of disability justice in upholding Indigenous voice that articulates disability and conceptions of justice from Indigenous epistemology and lived conditions. See Alice Wong, *Disability Visibility: First-Person Stories from the Twenty-First Century* (New York: Vintage Books, 2020).

12 Alice Wong, *Disability Visibility: First-Person Stories from the Twenty-First Century* (New York: Vintage Books, 2020), xx.

13 Amber Dion advocates for the "language of possibility" in Indigenous research, by thinking of pathways forward for Indigenous peoples. See Amber Dion, "Ahcâhk Recognizing Spirit," Indigenous Transdisciplinary Research Series, webinar, Auckland, New Zealand, October 26, 2021, https://www.facebook.com/watch/?v=938597713462703.

14 Committed to Diné methodology, I intentionally centered Diné theorizing of the world and disability. Although theorizing power relations and mapping settler-colonialism histories are important for critical Indigenous scholarship, for this article, I instead turned attention toward articulating possibilities of the

future rather than responding to systems of oppression. See Linda Tuhiwai Smith, *Decolonizing Methodologies*, 2nd ed. (London: Zed Books, 2012).

15 Māori scholars such as Linda Tuhiwai-Smith, Te Kawehau Hoskins, and Melinda Webber all argue that although critique is valuable and necessary, it is also important to think generatively and world build outside of the abusive and biopolitical relations with colonizing structures. Constantly responding to colonizing histories, logics, and discourse keeps Indigenous peoples busy from doing the important work of rebuilding their worlds. This refusal is a political act that dedicates to building relations with Indigenous communities, land, and knowledge as a critical site for engagement.

16 Lloyd Lee, *Diné Identity in a Twenty-First Century World* (University of Arizona Press, 2020).

17 Chad Pfeiffer, Diné, Albuquerque, storytelling and protocol, personal communication, December 18, 2021.

18 Herman Cody, "Diné Early Childhood Cultural Practices and Teachings," Diné Early Childhood Summit: Practice and Teachings, webinar, August 25, 2021.

19 Lorenzo Jim, "Healing through Storytelling," Center for Intercultural Care, webinar, March 22, 2022.

20 Lorenzo Jim, "Children Are Sacred," Office of Native and Spiritual Medicine, Center for Intercultural Care, webinar, March 15, 2022.

21 Viola Cordova, Kathleen Moore and Theodore Jojola, *How It Was: The Native American Philosophy V.T. Cordova*, (Tucson: University of Arizona Press, 2007).

22 Lloyd Lee, *Diné Perspectives: Revitalizing and Reclaiming Navajo Thought* (Tucson: University of Arizona Press, 2014).

23 Chad Pfeiffer, Diné, Albuquerque, storytelling and protocol, personal communication, December 18, 2021.

24 Sandra Yellowhorse, "My Tongue is a Mountain: Land, Belonging and the Politics of Voice," *Genealogy* 4, no. 4 (2020): 14, *http://dx.doi.org/10.3390/ genealogy4040112*.

25 Chad Pfeiffer, Diné, Albuquerque, storytelling, personal communication, February 2018.

26 This term is considered a sacred term, which Diné do not use lightly. In fact, we are taught not to say it too many times and without care for the implications of what it means to say it. Therefore, it is abbreviated throughout this paper. See Lloyd Lee, "Navajo Identity," guest lecture, University of New Mexico, Department of Music and Department of American Studies, February 2015.

27 Lloyd Lee, *Diné Perspectives: Revitalizing and Reclaiming Navajo Thought* (Tucson: University of Arizona Press, 2014), 3.

28 See Vincent Werito, "Understanding Hózhó to Achieve Critical Consciousness: A Contemporary Diné Interpretation of the Philosophical Principles of Hózhó," in *Diné Perspectives: Revitalizing and Reclaiming Navajo Thought* (Tucson: University of Arizona Press, 2014); and Lloyd Lee, *Diné Perspectives: Revitalizing and Reclaiming Navajo Thought* (Tucson: University of Arizona Press, 2014), 3, 5.

29 See Vangee Nez, "Diné Epistemology: Sa'ah Naaghái

Bik'eh Hózhóón Teachings," PhD dissertation, University of New Mexico, 2018, *https://digitalrepository .unm.edu/educ_llss_etds/92/*; and Herbert Benally, "Navajo Philosophy of Learning and Pedagogy," PhD dissertation, Northern Arizona University, 1994.

30 Vangee Nez, " Diné Epistemology: Sa'ah Naaghái Bik'eh Hózhóón Teachings," PhD dissertation, University of New Mexico, 2018, *https://digitalrepository .unm.edu/educ_llss_etds/92/*; and Lloyd Lee, *Diné Perspectives: Revitalizing and Reclaiming Navajo Thought* (Tucson: University of Arizona Press, 2014).

31 Lloyd Lee, *Diné Perspectives: Revitalizing and Reclaiming Navajo Thought* (Tucson: University of Arizona Press, 2014); and Vincent Werito, "Understanding Hózhó to Achieve Critical Consciousness: A Contemporary Diné Interpretation of the Philosophical Principles of Hózhó," in *Diné Perspectives: Revitalizing and Reclaiming Navajo Thought* (Tucson: University of Arizona Press, 2014), 25–38.

32 Ibid.

33 Vincent Werito, "Understanding Hózhó to Achieve Critical Consciousness: A Contemporary Diné Interpretation of the Philosophical Principles of Hózhó," in *Diné Perspectives: Revitalizing and Reclaiming Navajo Thought* (Tucson: University of Arizona Press, 2014), 26.

34 Found in Lloyd Lee, *Diné Perspectives: Revitalizing and Reclaiming Navajo Thought* (Tucson: University of Arizona Press, 2014), 7.

35 Lloyd Lee, *Diné Perspectives: Revitalizing and Reclaiming Navajo Thought* (Tucson: University of Arizona Press, 2014).

36 Vincent Werito, "Understanding Hózhó to Achieve Critical Consciousness: A Contemporary Diné Interpretation of the Philosophical Principles of Hózhó," in *Diné Perspectives: Revitalizing and Reclaiming Navajo Thought* (Tucson: University of Arizona Press, 2014), 25–38; and Lloyd Lee, *Diné Perspectives: Revitalizing and Reclaiming Navajo Thought* (Tucson: University of Arizona Press, 2014).

37 Lloyd Lee, *Diné Perspectives: Revitalizing and Reclaiming Navajo Thought* (Tucson: University of Arizona Press, 2014), 6.

38 Vincent Werito, "Understanding Hózhó to Achieve Critical Consciousness: A Contemporary Diné Interpretation of the Philosophical Principles of Hózhó," in *Diné Perspectives: Revitalizing and Reclaiming Navajo Thought* (Tucson: University of Arizona Press, 2014), 25–38.

39 Ibid., 26.

40 Ibid., 33.

41 Ibid., 25–38.

42 Diné scholars Farina King and Tammy Yonnie describe the four-directions paradigm as a compass. See Farina King, *The Earth Memory Compass: Diné Landscapes and Education in the Twentieth Century* (Lawrence: University Press of Kansas, 2018); and Tammy Yonnie, "Traditional Navajo Storytelling as an Educational Strategy," PhD dissertation, Arizona State University, 2016, https://hdl.handle.net/2286/R.I.41247.

43 Wilson Aronilth Jr., *Foundations of Navajo Culture*, 1st draft published for 1985 edition (Tsaile, AZ: Navajo Community College, 1985).

44 Cited in Ester Belin, Jeff Berglund, Connie A. Jacobs, and Anthony

K. Webster, *The Diné Reader: An Anthology of Navajo Literature* (Tucson: University of Arizona Press, 2021), 12.

45 Kevin Belin, "Journey of the Hero Twins to Their Father," NACA Storyteller Series, webinar, Albuquerque, New Mexico, February 5, 2021.

46 Vincent Werito, "Understanding Hózhó to Achieve Critical Consciousness: A Contemporary Diné Interpretation of the Philosophical Principles of Hózhó," in *Diné Perspectives: Revitalizing and Reclaiming Navajo Thought* (Tucson: University of Arizona Press, 2014), 25–38.

47 Manley Begay, "The Path of Navajo Sovereignty in Traditional Education: Harmony, Disruption, Distress and Restoration of Harmony," in *Navajo Sovereignty* (Tucson: University of Arizona Press, 2018), 60.

48 Vincent Werito, "Understanding Hózhó to Achieve Critical Consciousness: A Contemporary Diné Interpretation of the Philosophical Principles of Hózhó," in *Diné Perspectives: Revitalizing and Reclaiming Navajo Thought* (Tucson: University of Arizona Press, 2014), 27.

49 Farina King, *The Earth Memory Compass: Diné Landscapes and Education in the Twentieth Century* (Lawrence: University Press of Kansas, 2018).

50 Alberta Curley, "Navajo Wellness Model," Warrior Wednesday, Navajo Nation Division of Behavioral & Mental Health, Facebook Live, September 9, 2020, *https://www.facebook.com/422648268566903/videos/634845210503226/?__so__=channel_tab&__rv__=all_videos_card*.

51 Vincent Werito, "Understanding Hózhó to Achieve Critical

Consciousness: A Contemporary Diné Interpretation of the Philosophical Principles of Hózhó," in *Diné Perspectives: Revitalizing and Reclaiming Navajo Thought* (Tucson: University of Arizona Press, 2014), 34.

52 Sandra Yellowhorse, "My Tongue Is a Mountain: Land, Belonging and the Politics of Voice," *Genealogy* 4, no. 4 (2020), http://dx.doi.org/10.3390/genealogy4040112.

53 Lloyd Lee, Diné, Homeland terminology, Albuquerque, personal communication, February 2022.

54 Wilson Aronilth Jr., *Foundations of Navajo Culture*, 1st draft published for 1985 edition (Tsaile, AZ: Navajo Community College, 1985); and Evangeline Parsons-Yazzie and Margaret Speas, *Diné Bizaad Bínáhoo'aah: Rediscovering the Navajo Language* (Flagstaff, AZ: Salina Bookshelf Publishing, 2007).

55 Kevin Belin, "Journey of the Hero Twins to Their Father," NACA Storyteller Series, webinar, Albuquerque, New Mexico, February 5, 2021.

56 Irvin Morris, *From the Glittering World: A Navajo Story* (Norman: University of Oklahoma Press, 1997).

57 Jake Skeets, "NEA Big Read Poetry Night Kickoff : Evening Song," Virginia G. Piper Center for Creative Writing, April 19, 2021, https://youtu.be/dPZKjcJUzmM; Manley Begay "The Path of Navajo Sovereignty in Traditional Education: Harmony, Disruption, Distress and Restoration of Harmony," in *Navajo Sovereignty* (Tucson: University of Arizona Press, 2018), 57–90; Wilson Aronilth Jr., *Foundations of Navajo Culture*, 1st draft published for 1985 edition (Tsaile, AZ: Navajo Community

College, 1985); and Lorenzo Jim, "Healing Through Storytelling," Center for Intercultural Care, webinar, March 22, 2022.

58 Mary Hasbah Roessel, "Diné Youth Living in Two Worlds: Teachings from the Hooghan and How It Provided the Foundation for a Diné Psychiatrist," Diné Studies Conference, Tsalie, Arizona, June 25, 2021, https://dinestudies.org/2021_day1morning_session2.

59 Wilson Aronilth Jr., *Foundations of Navajo Culture*, 1st draft published for 1985 edition (Tsaile, AZ: Navajo Community College, 1985).

60 Vincent Werito, "Understanding Hózhó to Achieve Critical Consciousness: A Contemporary Diné Interpretation of the Philosophical Principles of Hózhó," in *Diné Perspectives: Revitalizing and Reclaiming Navajo Thought* (Tucson: University of Arizona Press, 2014), 30, 32.

61 Jake Skeets, "NEA Big Read Poetry Night Kickoff : Evening Song," Virginia G. Piper Center for Creative Writing, April 19, 2021, https://youtu.be/dPZKjcJUzmM.

62 Vincent Werito, "Understanding Hózhó to Achieve Critical Consciousness: A Contemporary Diné Interpretation of the Philosophical Principles of Hózhó," in *Diné Perspectives: Revitalizing and Reclaiming Navajo Thought* (Tucson: University of Arizona Press, 2014), 25–38.

63 Dinétah differs from Diné Bikéyah (Navajo Land). Dinétah is the territory that Diné were born of and to. The logics that underwrite this understanding of land comes from inherent belonging to the land articulated through our origin stories (Morris, 1997). Diné Bikéyah is

governed by cartography that emerged from the Treaty of 1868, where the US government decided what lands Diné people would occupy. Belonging and reciprocal claiming of land and land which claims us in return are articulated through the designation of Dinétah as relative to ancestral territory predicated on Diné story and not colonial mapping processes.

64 Evangeline Parsons-Yazzie and Margaret Speas, *Diné Bizaad Bínáhoo'aah: Rediscovering the Navajo Language* (Flagstaff, AZ: Salina Bookshelf Publishing, 2007).

65 Wilson Aronilth Jr., *Foundations of Navajo Culture*, 1st draft published for 1985 edition (Tsaile, AZ: Navajo Community College, 1985).

66 Evangeline Parsons-Yazzie and Margaret Speas, *Diné Bizaad Bínáhoo'aah: Rediscovering the Navajo Language* (Flagstaff, AZ: Salina Bookshelf Publishing, 2007).

67 Tammy Yonnie, "Traditional Navajo Storytelling as an Educational Strategy," PhD dissertation, Arizona State University, 2016, https://hdl.handle.net/2286/R.I.41247.

68 Vincent Werito, "Understanding Hózhó to Achieve Critical Consciousness: A Contemporary Diné Interpretation of the Philosophical Principles of Hózhó," in *Diné Perspectives: Revitalizing and Reclaiming Navajo Thought* (Tucson: University of Arizona Press, 2014), 25–38.

69 Tifa Rain, Diné Relational Model, 2022, digital media. Consultation with Saad Kidilyé, Diné Language Nest.

70 Mary Hasbah Roessel, "Diné Youth Living in Two Worlds: Teachings from the Hooghan and How It Provided the Foundation for a Diné Psychiatrist," Diné Studies Conference, Tsalie, Arizona, June 25, 2021, https://dinestudies.org/2021_day1morning_session2.

71 Teachings of weaving often convey how the loom encases its own world, which relates to larger lifeways. See Luci Tapahonso, "NEA Big Read Poetry Night Kickoff: Evening Song," Virginia G. Piper Center for Creative Writing, April 19, 2021, https://youtu.be/dPZKjcJUzmM; and Noel Bennett, *Navajo Weaving Way: From Fleece to the Rug* (Loveland, CO: Interweave Publishers, 1997).

72 For further reading on the concept of wholeness, see Wilson Aronilth Jr., *Foundations of Navajo Culture*, 1st draft published for 1985 edition (Tsaile, AZ: Navajo Community College, 1985).

73 Ibid.

74 Lloyd Lee, *Diné Perspectives: Revitalizing and Reclaiming Navajo Thought* (Tucson: University of Arizona Press, 2014), 5.

75 Farina King, *The Earth Memory Compass: Diné Landscapes and Education in the Twentieth Century* (Lawrence: University Press of Kansas, 2018); and Tammy Yonnie, "Traditional Navajo Storytelling as an Educational Strategy," PhD dissertation, Arizona State University, 2016, https://hdl.handle.net/2286/R.I.41247.

76 Vincent Werito, "Understanding Hózhó to Achieve Critical Consciousness: A Contemporary Diné Interpretation of the Philosophical Principles of Hózhó," in *Diné Perspectives: Revitalizing and Reclaiming Navajo Thought* (Tucson: University of Arizona Press, 2014), 33.

77 Ibid., 34.

78 Ibid., 34.

79 Ibid., 34.

80 Ibid., 34.

81 Kevin Belin, "Journey of the Hero Twins to Their Father," NACA Storyteller Series, webinar, Albuquerque, New Mexico, February 5, 2021.

82 Chad Pfeiffer, Diné, Albuquerque, storytelling, personal communication, February 2018.

83 Vincent Werito, "Understanding Hózhó to Achieve Critical Consciousness: A Contemporary Diné Interpretation of the Philosophical Principles of Hózhó," in Diné Perspectives: Revitalizing and Reclaiming Navajo Thought (Tucson: University of Arizona Press, 2014), 29.

84 Lloyd Lee, Diné Perspectives: Revitalizing and Reclaiming Navajo Thought (Tucson: University of Arizona Press, 2014).

85 Ibid.

86 Gregory Cajete, Look to the Mountain: An Ecology of Indigenous Education (Ontario: Kivaki Press, 1994).

87 Johnathan Tautari, Pou Ārahi, Auckaland, Māori understandings of disability and autonomy, personal communication, 2019; Gregory Cajete, Indigenous Community: Rekindling the Teachings of the Seventh Fire (Minneapolis: Living Justice Press, 2015).

88 Theorized using Klopfenstein's analysis of k'é and relationships as a medium of knowing and placing into conversation with dialogue of individual and community relationality. Adair Klopfenstein, "How You Relate to Everything is the Key to Living Your Life," Leading the Way: The Wisdom of the Navajo People, February 2021, 7–9.

89 Lloyd Lee, Diné Perspectives: Revitalizing and Reclaiming Navajo Thought (Tucson: University of Arizona Press, 2014).

90 Lloyd Lee, Diné Identity in a 21st-Century World (Tucson: University of Arizona Press, 2020), 70.

91 Wilson Aronilth Jr., Foundations of Navajo Culture, 1st draft published for 1985 edition (Tsaile, AZ: Navajo Community College, 1985).

92 Avery Denny, "Exploring the Diné Map of the Stars: Navajo Astronomy 101; #Be Powerful Diné Culture Camp," Iina Bihoo'aah, Facebook Live, January 27, 2022, https://www.facebook.com/iinabihooaah/videos/931843267722431; and Wilson Aronilth Jr., Foundations of Navajo Culture, 1st draft published for 1985 edition (Tsaile, AZ: Navajo Community College, 1985).

93 Evangeline Parsons-Yazzie and Margaret Speas, Diné Bizaad Bínáhoo'aah: Rediscovering the Navajo Language (Flagstaff, AZ: Salina Bookshelf Publishing, 2007), 70.

94 Wilson Aronilth Jr., Foundations of Navajo Culture, 1st draft published for 1985 edition (Tsaile, AZ: Navajo Community College, 1985).

95 Jake Skeets, "NEA Big Read Poetry Night Kickoff: Evening Song," Virginia G. Piper Center for Creative Writing, April 19, 2021, https://youtu.be/dPZKjcJUzmM.

96 Larry Emerson, "Diné Culture, Decolonization and the Politics of Hózhó," in Dine Perspective: Revitalizing and Reclaiming Navajo Thought (Tucson: University of Arizona Press, 2014), 49–67.

97 Vincent Werito, "Understanding Hózhó to Achieve Critical Consciousness: A Contemporary Diné Interpretation of the Philosophical Principles of Hózhó," in Diné Perspectives:

Revitalizing and Reclaiming Navajo Thought (Tucson: University of Arizona Press, 2014), 33.

98 See Huhana Hickey, "Tātau tātau: Engaging with whanau hauā from within a Cultural Framework," in *Working with Māori Children with Special Education Needs: He mahi whakahirahira* (NZCER Press, 2015).

99 Lloyd Lee, *Diné Perspectives: Revitalizing and Reclaiming Navajo Thought* (Tucson: University of Arizona Press, 2014), 5–6.

100 Talila Lewis (2020) outlines in her definition on systemic ableism as value "based on societally constructed ideas of normality, intelligence, excellence, desirable and productivity . . . rooted in anti-Blackness, eugenics, misogyny, colonialism, imperialism and capitalism." See Talilia Lewis, "Ableism 2022: An Updated Definition," blog, January 25, 2020, https://

www.talilalewis.com/blog/ableism-2020-an-updated-definition.

101 See Harriet McBryde Johnson, "Unspeakable Conversations," in *Disabilty Visibility* (Vintage Books, 2020), 3–27.

102 See Sandra Yellowhorse, "Disability and Indigenous Resistance: Mapping Value Politics During the Time of COVID-19," *AlterNative* (2022), https://doi.org/10.1177/1177180122112332.

103 Gregory Cajete, *Look to the Mountain: An Ecology of Indigenous Education* (Ontario: Kivaki Press, 1994).

104 Amber Dion, "Ahcâhk Recognizing Spirit," Indigenous Transdisciplinary Research Series, webinar, Auckland, New Zealand, October 26, 2021, https://www.facebook.com/watch/?v=938597713462703.

Narratives of Indigenous Women Leaders
Indigenous-Centered Approaches to Leadership

Heather J. Shotton and Robin Zape-tah-hol-ah Minthorn

Indigenous women have historically held important places in our tribal societies. We know that our women are powerful, we recognize and respect the important places they hold, as Indigenous people we understand our histories, and Indigenous women as leaders is nothing new to us. In our traditional tribal societies Indigenous women played important roles, and it was not uncommon for Indigenous women to hold spiritual, political, and economic power.[1] Women carried "many responsibilities including choosing tribal leaders, deciding on when to go to war, and determining the fate of captives."[2] Unfortunately, the broader scholarship on Indigenous people has largely ignored the central role of and leadership roles held by Indigenous women. A number of scholars have been critical of the absence of Indigenous women and our voices in the scholarship.[3]

Indigenous scholar Devon Mihesuah has critiqued previous scholarship for its failure to include the voices of Indigenous women and for the ways that colonialism affects how Indigenous women are portrayed in the scholarship.[4] She points to the problematic nature of colonizers writing about Indigenous people, calling attention to the pitfalls of using colonial standards to interpret the cultures, histories, and experiences of Indigenous people. She explains that "A common complaint throughout the world's Indigenous communities is that colonizers have barged into these communities and written what they pleased about the people and cultures with no regard for what the subjects have to say about it."[5] Moreover, the scholarship on Indigenous women has historically failed to address our modern roles and realities. Mihesuah offers a sharp critique of the extant scholarship on Indigenous women for its failings to connect to the present and for ignoring the complexity of Indigenous women.[6] And there remains a need for scholarship that explores and honors the place that Indigenous women hold as leaders and our contributions to the survival of Indigenous communities.[7]

Indigenous women continue to remain central figures in our tribes and communities and they fulfill important roles as leaders, activists, educators, and scholars. Unfortunately, the scholarship remains limited on the experiences and unique perspectives of Indigenous women in leadership positions. Our understanding of their involvement in specific organizations or movements, their journeys to leadership, and the values that guide their leadership is severely lacking. Through a study of fifteen contemporary Indigenous women leaders, we sought to explore the perspectives of Indigenous women leaders. This article presents findings from this study and specifically examines the role of cultural values in the development and approaches of Indigenous women leaders. We seek to fill a significant gap in the scholarship pertaining to Indigenous women and provide important insight into Indigenous women's leadership perspectives.

INDIGENOUS LEADERSHIP

The literature on leadership and leadership development is expansive; however the broader scholarship fails to incorporate Indigenous perspectives on leadership. Robin Minthorn asserts that understanding the constructs of Indigenous leadership is important in examining Indigenous leaders.[8] The literature that addresses Indigenous leadership is limited, but provides important insight into Indigenous leadership values. Scholars have identified three major factors that shape Indigenous perspectives of leadership: cultural identity, community engagement and social responsibility, and leadership values.

Tanya Fitzgerald addresses the challenge of developing a universal definition of Indigenous leadership, explaining that Indigenous leadership is exercised in varying ways.[9] What Fitzgerald suggests is that there are two layers of Indigenous leadership: (1) traditional, or community, leadership that derives from an Indigenous worldview; and (2) leadership that serves as advocacy between Indigenous and non-Indigenous communities.[10] The community engagement and social responsibility component of Indigenous leadership is an integral part of the Native American community.[11] Tarrell Portman and Michael

Garrett affirm that shared vision and responsibility are foundational values of Indigenous leadership.[12] Lawrence Wise-Erickson examines the congruency between team-based leadership and the values of Native American leadership within tribal communities, and finds congruence between the values and the need to create a community-based leadership model that integrates the roles, values, and holistic nature of the Indigenous communities and concepts of leadership.[13] Consequently, exploring how to create a sense of understanding between Indigenous and non-Indigenous populations, with regard to community engagement and social responsibility, is essential.

Recently, a few key studies have begun to explore contemporary Indigenous women and leadership. In a study of nine Indigenous women leaders, Denise Lajimodiere identified key characteristics and experiences of Indigenous women leaders.[14] Findings from this study point to the important roles of support networks, the importance of tribal culture and spirituality, and resiliency in leadership for Indigenous women. Lajimodeire also identified issues of gender bias from men and sabotaging from other women as an experience for the women in her study.[15] Portman and Garrett found that patience, listening, contemplating the situation, and developing innovative strategies to accomplish tasks are skills employed by Indigenous women leaders.[16] They further assert the importance of mentorship of Indigenous female leaders in an environment of collectivism. In a study of more than one hundred Native women leaders, Tippeconnic Fox et al. found that cultural values of respect, humility, trust, relationships, commitment to community, generosity, courage, and honoring of traditional female roles are important for Native women leaders.[17] They assert that Native women leaders embrace both traditional Native leadership skills and values and nontraditional leadership skills in their roles as leaders.

Despite the emerging, albeit limited, scholarship on Indigenous women leaders, there remains a need for more scholarship that privileges our voices and perspectives. Scholars continue to call for research that honors the power of Indigenous women to tell our own stories and define our own realities.[18]

METHODS

This study employed a qualitative approach that was guided by an Indigenous research paradigm. The purpose of our study was to explore the experiences and perspectives of Indigenous women in leadership, so we felt that it was imperative to approach this research in a way that was guided by Indigenous values that privileged Indigenous women's voices; the utilization of an Indigenous research paradigm was fitting for this purpose. This approach allowed for our research to be strengthened by inherent Indigenous knowledge, values, and lived experiences. More importantly, an Indigenous research paradigm approach is based on the supposition that the research is not being conducted *on* people or participants, but *with* participants.[19]

The personal narratives of fifteen Indigenous female leaders served as the data source for this study, which was guided by the following research question: What are the experiences of Indigenous female leaders? In order to gain a better understanding of the research question, the following sub-questions were addressed:

How do Indigenous women approach leadership?
How do Indigenous women view themselves as leaders?
How do leadership roles impact Indigenous women?
In what context do Indigenous women serve in leadership?

DATA COLLECTION

Data was collected through one-on-one, in-depth interviews with fifteen Indigenous female leaders from across the United States. A standardized interview protocol was utilized for all interviews, but interviews were conducted in an informal manner that allowed for flexibility. Interviews were guided by a set of eight open-ended questions that allowed participants to focus on their personal experiences and share their stories of leadership as Indigenous women.

Interviews were conducted in a personal space chosen by the women where they felt comfortable (e.g., their homes, hotel rooms, or private offices). It was important that we traveled to the participants and conducted the interviews in a manner that allowed for their comfort as a mechanism of relationality. As Indigenous researchers who were familiar with many of the women in this study, it was also important that we spent time reestablishing our connections with participants prior to beginning each interview. Interviews typically lasted between one and two hours and were audio recorded and transcribed for accuracy.

Purposive sampling was utilized for this study. We sought women who identify as Indigenous, who serve in various leadership roles, and who are recognized in the broader Native community as leaders. The women who are represented in this study identify as Indigenous and represent various tribal nations from within the United States. They each serve in various leadership roles (e.g., tribal government, education administration, non-profit, state legislature).

DATA ANALYSIS

Data analysis occurred in four stages. First, as a matter of member checking, transcripts were sent to participants to review for accuracy.

After participants reviewed transcripts, each researcher independently read through the transcripts to identify initial codes. The researchers then came together to verify and agree on a set of codes; any discrepancies between codes were noted and resolved.[20] Six codes were identified and transcripts were coded manually in an effort to gain familiarity with the data. Once all transcripts were coded, the data were reexamined to ensure accuracy and codes were further collapsed into themes. The themes that emerged from the data are discussed in the following section.

FINDINGS

Findings from this study indicate that leadership for the women in this study was centered in Indigenous values that were garnered from the communities in which they grew up, as well as the values instilled in them by their grandparents, parents, and families. The tribal values of each of the women greatly influenced them in their lifeways and in their leadership positions. The values that emerged were being of service to their communities, mentoring and providing pathways for others, and the importance of honesty, humility, and loyalty. Furthermore, the women often discussed the journey to leadership as unplanned and the term "leadership" did not resonate with them; instead, notions of service and community building were more fitting. Their perspectives on their roles as leaders were not focused on them as individuals; rather, their focus was on how they might benefit others.

Community and Familial Influence

TRIBAL COMMUNITIES

The narratives of the women in this study consistently pointed to their connections to their tribal communities. Each of the women identified themselves through their clans, tribal names, and the connections they have to them. They spoke about their clanship, connections to their communities, the values that were taught to them by their elders, and how each of those influences their approaches to leadership. One woman explained that being raised by her grandmother provided important teachings for her that reminded her not to compromise who she is. Another woman connected her leadership to her clan, explaining:

> I think the other thing is that mainstream defines leadership. I think completely different than how you aspire to leadership as a Native person. I actually think in Indigenous cultures you sort of are just born to be a leader. I know that's so cliché but one of the things that I was told is that even my own clan's identity I have one of the clan identities that is about leadership. The trait of that clan

is that you're a leader and when I learned that I was really feeling like, wow, okay. I felt like they were telling me that because they were saying that's your responsibility now whereas I never really thought about that before.

The women drew distinct connections between their leadership and their tribal identities. Moreover, connections to their communities were evident in their desire to serve their tribal communities and the broader Indigenous community. In their professional backgrounds each woman has either worked directly with their own tribal communities or found ways to work with the broader Indigenous community.

Tribal identity is central for Indigenous people, and for Indigenous women it is largely understood that they are defined primarily by their tribal identities.[21] So, it is not surprising that among the women that were a part of this study their connections to their tribal communities were an important part of their leadership.

FAMILIAL INFLUENCE

Relationships are central to Indigenous epistemologies and understandings of relationships are critical to an individual's sense of self and understanding of their place in the community. Particularly, familial ties and relationships are viewed as sacred. The women in this study spoke extensively about the role of family in shaping their identity as leaders. Their discussions about family included grandparents, parents, siblings, children, and grandchildren. Grandparents held a special place for the women in this study, as many of them spoke to the special role that their grandparents' teaching held for them. One woman explained the critical role of her grandmother's teachings in her leadership:

> Also what I behold I guess in my own cultural way of having been taught to be a Native woman. Sometimes when I come to situations where I sort of have that moment of this is right; should I do this, should I say this, should I be thinking this? I always draw on what would my grandmother think? What would my grandmother say? Would I do this in front of my grandmother? That really brings you back to okay, stay grounded.

Additionally, the women discussed how they extend the value of family to their work. One of the women explained that she extends the value of family to her leadership role in the way that she approaches the people with whom she works: "Value family and letting them also, letting them, giving them the time and think it's okay if you need to take care of your mom, your dad within reason, we will understand." Having a consciousness of balancing these familial roles in combination with their leadership roles was a priority.

Tribal Values

LEADERSHIP AS SERVICE

An important finding in this study was that leadership was defined as service. Each of the women discussed their leadership in a way that embodies a deep value for service and fulfilling necessary roles. In fact, they were hesitant to label themselves as leaders, and spoke of the work that they do as "being of service." Their professional work was centered on serving their own tribal communities, Indigenous people, or Indian country more broadly. One of the women described her value of service through her leadership at a tribal college:

> I feel like this school is owed to our people. It is a sovereign right. It is a treaty right. If we let it fail, we fail our people. That's how strongly I feel, I feel that we owe it to our Indian people to work hard, work as hard as we can mind, body, and soul to get this school to a place where our Indian people will be proud of.

Service was also discussed in the context of tribal ceremonies, and the women referenced the sacrifices made during ceremonies as sacred and an example of teachings from elders that guided their approaches to leadership. Service and filling necessary roles is a value that is embodied in how the women approached their roles in their communities and in their professional leadership roles. They discussed service as a cultural value that is carried out daily in the ways that they approach both their professional and family lives.

HUMILITY

Another value that emerged from this study was that of humility. The women in this study were reluctant to call themselves leaders and found it difficult to discuss their roles in terms of leadership; instead, as stated above, they spoke about their work as being of service. They spoke freely about their paths to leadership and mentors or family members who made a way for them, but they were very humble about sharing their specific contributions and roles as leaders. They discussed their contributions as leaders in terms of simply doing the work that needed to be done. For instance, one of the women said, "In terms of leadership, I don't know if it was something that I sought that I cannot stand to sit by and see mediocrity and when there's work to do, you just roll your sleeves up and you just pitch in, you just do what needs to be done." For the women in this study, status was not a consideration or motivator in the work that they did as leaders; their motivation was rooted in doing the work for the sake of the community. They were not concerned with who received credit for the work. What arose from the narratives was that acknowledging leadership as an Indigenous person is not about the individual, but rather the collective. One woman explained:

> The other one I think that's absolutely key, I could not have done anything that I've done without a team . . . the collective wisdom of a group was just phenomenal . . . I think that speaks to the heart of leadership. You're not a leader unless you've got people working with you. It's not all about one person.

A part of the role of being a Native woman leader is having the humility to not worry about your status, but the work that is being done for the broader community. Furthermore, many of the women's views of leadership reflected beliefs that individuals are chosen to be leaders because of qualities that they possess; that is, one does not necessarily decide that they will serve in a leadership role; such things are decided by the broader community.

MENTORING

In each of the stories shared by the Native women in this study, it was apparent that each had been mentored by someone or given an opportunity because someone believed in them. Each of the women recognized this and expressed the importance of mentoring. One woman discussed the importance of mentorship in her role as a tribal college president:

> I feel like what I have entrusted in me as the president is I have to be a good role model. I have to show the students that if I can do it, you can. I also have to portray to them honesty, the good traits, the positive traits. Learn to appreciate the people around you, say hello to them, give them a hug, treat them well, treat them with respect.
> I think for me that's the most powerful person I can be is to be a good example of what a person can be. Share, share with each other. Be gracious, be grateful. For me this gives me that opportunity to do that. The other part of it is along with growing the next generation type of leaders I think the other part of it has to do with sovereignty.

In their own experiences they realized the important role of mentorship, as well as the impact that their leadership roles have on future generations, particularly young Native women. One woman explained,

"We have responsibilities to young girls, who, whether we like it or not, we are role modeling some things for them." This insight demonstrates the uniqueness of being an Indigenous woman leader, as role modeling and focus on future generations was a central theme. One woman stated, "What are we doing, not only to carry forward that moment in DC, but carry forward the next generations, because I want [my granddaughter's] children to have these opportunities and I want her to know what her tribe means." Each woman expressed that they understood the importance of their role as a leader and their responsibility to impact youth, young professionals, young women, and colleagues. The value of mentorship to them was imbedded in their stories and narratives.

Discussion

Indigenous women have historically held important positions in our tribal communities, and they continue to play important roles today as leaders in tribal governance, national organizations, educational institutions, and federal and state government. However, we have yet to fully examine the experiences of Indigenous women in leadership and our understanding of the role of tribal culture remains limited; this study provides insight into this phenomenon. Findings from this study serve to help us better understand the experiences of Indigenous women in leadership and have important implications for research and practice.

Findings from this study clearly indicate that there is a difference in how leadership is conceptualized from an Indigenous perspective. These findings are consistent with previous research that indicates that leadership and values of leadership are perceived differently when viewed through an Indigenous lens. Indigenous values were key in how the women in this study approached and experienced leadership. Leadership was not approached from an individual perspective; rather, it was distinctly tied to community, family, and service.[22] Findings on community approaches to leadership support previous research focused on Indigenous women leaders and indicate that values of commitment to community, family, and service to the greater good are central to Indigenous women's perspectives of leadership.[23]

Findings from this study further expanded Indigenous leadership values of service and commitment to community and indicate that mentorship is a central value. Each of the women in this study indicated that they benefited from mentoring and that mentorship was key in their development as leaders. They acknowledged that they had benefited greatly from their mentors and as a result felt a responsibility to mentor others. Mentoring for them was an intentional act and they actively sought out other Indigenous people, particularly other Indigenous women, to mentor. The desire to mentor others went beyond the notion of giving back, and was more related to the responsibility of creating paths that contributed to the greater good of the community. This finding is consistent with previous findings from Portman and Garrett and has important implications for future research with regard to Indigenous views of mentorship as a responsibility to future generations and nation building.[24]

Findings from this study point to the need for further research on mentoring relationships for Indigenous women. The women in this study indicated that mentors were both male and female, Indigenous and non-Indigenous, but mentors played a critical role in their experiences and development as leaders. Further examination is warranted to better understand how mentoring relationships in Indigenous leadership are developed and nurtured, and the specific roles they play for Indigenous women. Developing an understanding of how we can best cultivate intentional mentoring opportunities for Indigenous women is critical to future practice.

Findings also have important implications for how we support and develop Indigenous women as leaders. Important questions arise regarding how we work to foster intergenerational mentoring relationships. How do we work to identify potential leaders and provide opportunities to foster development of future leaders? How do we develop mechanisms to recognize those Indigenous leaders who can fill future roles and continue the cycle of leadership development to meet community needs? Now more than ever, we need community and tribal members who can help to build our communities and further nation-building efforts among our tribal nations. That means we must identify those who can support and foster our future leaders in schools and higher education institutions and those who will serve as advocates for our communities on a national level.

Finally, we must continue to deconstruct traditional Western notions of leadership and privilege Indigenous leadership values. Findings from this study point to distinct Indigenous perspectives of leadership that extend beyond the individual and are closely tied to Indigenous values of community and service. The women in this study repeatedly indicated that they did not seek out leadership positions; rather, their paths to leadership roles resulted from recognition of their leadership potential by others. Moreover, women in this study exhibited deep humility and were reluctant to call themselves leaders; rather, they viewed their positions as leaders as fulfilling a necessary role and being of service. Furthermore, we posit that this is connected to cultural notions that individuals are chosen to be leaders because of qualities that they possess; that is, one does not necessarily decide that they will serve in a leadership role, such things are decided by the broader community. Further exploration of this concept is necessary to better understand the notion of leaders as emergent.

The voices of contemporary Indigenous women have only recently begun to emerge in the scholarship. While previous scholarship offers important insight, it is imperative that we continue to develop a deeper understanding of the experiences of Indigenous women leaders. In a time when we continue to witness more Indigenous women assuming leadership positions in education, tribal governance, national organizations, and federal and state governance, it is safe to assume that Indigenous women will continue to play important roles in the leadership of Indigenous people, just as they always have. Our understanding of Indigenous women leaders is critical to our efforts to prepare future generations of Indigenous women leaders. Findings from this study have provided important insight into our understanding of leadership from an Indigenous female perspective and they build on previous scholarship. We have taken critical first steps to addressing how we understand and create future Indigenous female leaders and we urge further development of the scholarship on Indigenous women leaders.

AUTHOR BIOGRAPHIES

Dr. Heather J. Shotton is a citizen of the Wichita & Affiliated Tribes and is also of Kiowa and Cheyenne descent. She is the vice president of Diversity Affairs for Fort Lewis College.

Robin Zape-tah-hol-ah Minthorn, PhD (Kiowa/Umatilla/Nez Perce/Apache/Assiniboine), is an associate professor, director of the Educational Leadership Doctoral Program, and director of Indigenous Education Initiatives for the School of Education at the University of Washington Tacoma. She is the coeditor of the *Indigenous Leadership in Higher Education* book published by Routledge, *Reclaiming Indigenous Research in Higher Education and Indigenous Motherhood in the Academy* published by Rutgers University Press, and *Unsettling Settler Colonial Education: Transformational Indigenous Praxis Model* published by Teachers College Press.

NOTES

1 Denise K. Lajimodiere, "Ogimah Ikwe: Native Women and Their Path to Leadership," *Wicazo Sa Review* 26, no. 2 (2011): 57–82.

2 Mary Jo Tippeconic Fox, Eileen Luna-Firebaugh, and Caroline Williams, "American Indian Female Leadership," *Wicazo Sa Review* 30, no. 1 (2015): 83.

3 Elizabeth Cook-Lynn, *Why I Can't Read Wallace Stegner and Other Essays: A Tribal Voice* (Madison: University of Wisconsin Press, 1996); Devon A. Mihesuah, *Indigenous American Women: Decolonization, Empowerment, Activism* (Lincoln: University of Nebraska Press, 2003); Mary Jo Tippeconnic Fox, "American Indian Women in Academia:

The Joys and Challenges," *Journal About Women in Higher Education* 1 (2008): 202–21; Tippeconnic Fox et al., "American Indian Female Leadership," 82–99.

4 Mihesuah, *Indigenous American Women*, 36.

5 Ibid.

6 Mihesuah, *Indigenous American Women*, 3–4.

7 Tippeconnic Fox et al., "American Indian Female Leadership," 97.

8 Robin Minthorn, "Perspectives and Values of Leadership for Native American College Students in Non-Native Colleges and Universities," *Journal of Leadership Education* 12, no. 2 (2014): 67–95.

9 Tanya Fitzgerald, "Changing the Deafening Silence of Indigenous Women's Voices in Educational Leadership," *Journal of Educational Administration* 4, no. 1 (2003): 9–23.

10 Ibid.

11 Valorie Johnson, Maenette K. P. Benham, and Matthew VanAlstine, "Native Leadership: Advocacy for Transformation, Culture, Community, and Sovereignty," in *The Renaissance of American Indian Higher Education: Capturing the Dream*, ed. M. K. P. Benham and W. J. Stein (New York: Routledge, 2003), 149–66.

12 Tarrell A. Portman and Michael T. Garrett, "Beloved Women: Nurturing the Sacred Fire of Leadership from an American Indian Perspective," *Journal of Counseling & Development* 83 (2005): 284–91.

13 Lawrence Wise-Erickson, "Community-Based Leadership:

A Study of American Indian Leadership," PhD dissertation, Seattle University, 2003, 104–8.

14 Lajimodiere, "Ogimah Ikwe," 64.

15 Ibid., 70.

16 Portman and Garrett, "Beloved Women," 284–91.

17 Tippeconnic Fox et al., "American Indian Female Leadership," 82–99.

18 Fitzgerald, "Changing the Deafening Silence," 20; Mihesuah. *Indigenous American Women*, 37.

19 Shawn Wilson, *Research Is Ceremony: Indigenous Research Methods* (Manitoba, Canada: Fernwood Publishing Company, 2008), 77–79.

20 Matthew Miles, Michael Huberman, and Johnny Saldaña, *Qualitative Data Analysis: A Methods Sourcebook* (Thousand Oaks, CA: SAGE Publications, 2014), 55–68.

21 Paula Gunn Allen, *The Sacred Hoop: Recovering the Feminine in American Indian Traditions* (Boston: Beacon Press, 1986), 43.

22 Minthorn, "Perspectives and Values of Leadership," 67–95; Robin S. Williams, "Indigenizing Leadership Concepts Through Perspectives of Native American College Students," PhD dissertation, Oklahoma State University, 2012 (Order No., Oklahoma State University), ProQuest (3525658), 110.

23 Portman and Garrett, "Beloved Women," 287; Lajimodiere, "Ogimah Ikwe," 69; Tippeconnic Fox et al., "American Indian Female Leadership," 93.

24 Portman and Garrett, "Beloved Women," 286.

Using Stories to Teach

Aretha Matt

Igrew up on the Navajo reservation during the 1980s and 1990s. I attended a public school in a small rural community and graduated with about sixty other students. I left my home in Querino Canyon, Arizona, two weeks after graduation to attend a summer bridge program at Northern Arizona University in Flagstaff, Arizona. This program was designed to integrate students of color successfully into colleges and universities. Students selected for this program were also first-generation college students or students from low-income backgrounds. This program helped me to integrate successfully because they were intrusive and continued their support into my second year of college. I credit this program for my success as an undergraduate student because they provided the resources and support that I needed to acculturate and operate in a new academic environment. I faced challenges and setbacks as a college student; but I did not allow these to deter my decision to complete degrees, including a doctoral degree in English. Along the way, I found that many educators and administrators at colleges and universities were available and supportive when it came to acculturating students to the academic environment; however, I also learned that many of them lacked understanding about Native Americans and our cultures.

During my time as a graduate assistant instructor at the University of Arizona, Tucson, Arizona, I was categorized by faculty and graduate students on separate occasions as "quiet," "introverted," or "silent." They would also usually follow their remarks with a comment about how they had Native American students in their classes who, like me, were also quiet. They often reported that they did not know how to approach the student in a way that would open communication. Most Americans know little about Native Americans because our Native histories, stories, and experiences are ignored and/or silenced in schools across America. Most people know only what they learned in primary and secondary grades, which is limited to a paragraph, a page, or a chapter in an American history book or events that occur during Native American month. I felt compelled to teach fellow instructors and my peers about my upbringing and my Navajo (Diné) culture because I feared the lack of knowledge would cause them to develop stereotypical perspectives and other common misconceptions about their students. These instructors needed contextual knowledge to better assist their students. My quiet nature developed, in part, by how I grew up. Some Navajo parents, including my parents, taught their children that words carry weight and/or have creative power. This shaped how I interacted with others. I often heard elders say that it was important to think before we acted (or spoke). Because of this, I will always consider if what I will say will contribute in positive or negative ways to group discussions or one-on-one conversations. Elders, including my parents, reminded us that incessant talking was not looked well upon in the Navajo community because it called attention to self. My parents used shame tactics to correct me when I was overly talkative and boastful. Moreover, listening and observing were more esteemed qualities compared with speaking well. My family and other community leaders ingrained in us that learning was equivalent to listening and observing. There was an expectation that we could learn whatever was heard or observed. This way of learning taught me that my learning was *my* responsibility. I carried this learning style into my classes and was always a careful listener or observer—absorbing and retaining information. I rarely had questions to ask instructors because I was often still processing the lessons in my mind. I shared these kinds of facts and stories pertaining to my upbringing and my literacy practices to give other instructors some idea about my challenges as a Native American student and writer. I share the following story about my literacy journey to shed light on the challenges that some Native American students face on the pathway to literacy learning. This story is about me; however, it may compare to what other Native Americans, particularly Navajo students, have experienced.

I grew up understanding that stories impart knowledge. I learned early that storytelling helped us to understand the world. Navajos used stories as a reasoning method. We shared stories to remember, recognize, and revive knowledge. Navajos tell stories to entertain, inspire, remind, strengthen, and teach. When I sought out counsel from my parents or other community elders, I often found that they did not respond promptly with advice. They pondered for a brief period to gather their thoughts before responding; not with advice, but with a story that resembled my dilemma. The stories came from their lived experiences, other peoples' lived experiences, traditional Navajo stories, and/or the Holy Bible. The stories they shared had experiential knowledge, lessons learned, and morals. The unspoken expectation was that I might be inspired by the characters in these stories, be drawn to the morals and values inherent in these stories, and develop a foundation of knowledge to confidently make my own decisions.

Listening to stories developed my patience, listening skills, critical thinking abilities, analytical skills, and abilities to reflect. Storytelling helped me to understand my connection to family, the Navajo community, and Navajo history. Navajos pass down family history from generation to generation through stories about ancestors and elders. Additionally, our intricate Navajo clan system is kept intact through memory and stories. Cultural knowledge is kept alive by storytellers who retell the stories during the winter seasons or during ceremonies. The storytellers retain traditional stories with the intent of sharing them with future generations. Memory, then, is essential to this society. For the Navajos, sharing stories determines the survival of their traditions because their worldview and practices are embedded in stories. Navajos recognize the sacredness of stories. Stories have actively sustained the Navajos since time immemorial. Most stories, in general, have characters, a plotline, themes, and lessons learned. I grew up understanding that stories have clear meanings that can shape audience perceptions and shift atmospheres. Navajos believe and understand that their spoken words can shift moods, have influence over others, inspire ideas, and promote negative or positive results. For this reason, some stories are revered, and storytelling is esteemed. I purposely use storytelling and narratives in my teaching and writing and in my lectures and presentations because, for me, it is the most natural way of communicating my ideas.

Over the years, I have learned that other Navajos and others from different Native nations have comparable experiences to what I share in this narrative. For instance, "living in two worlds" is a notion many Native Americans understand and share. This idea can be applied to both physical and abstract spaces; some of these spaces are well defined and contested, while others are blurred and overlapping. "Living in two worlds" refers to non-Native and Native spaces that Native Americans traverse. This includes navigating English and Indigenous languages, living in both secular and spiritual spaces, and operating in dominant/subordinate spaces. Dominant/subordinate spaces are physical and abstract settings that have rules and standards established by the dominant group's culture and values and highlight their historical perception. These standards may often contend with the cultures and traditions of other groups. Academic environments and Western discourses are dominant/subordinate spaces because they function under stringent standards that align with Eurocentric ideals and favor a dominant groups' culture, while also subordinating the experiences, narratives, philosophies, and cultures of other groups. For example, most courses about American history will focus the narrative around colonizing the Americas, Western expansion, and establishing governments. However, Indigenous people, the inhabitants of the Americas, are left out of this narrative. Furthermore, Western modes of thought value concepts like linearity, classification of ideas, and structured or organized patterns. These modes may contend with Indigenous philosophies. For example, traditional Navajo worldview values circular/cyclical patterns of thought, communal objectives, and recognition and acceptance that life is dynamic or ever shifting. This means that Navajos, when moving across these discourse communities, will adopt and/or resist aspects from the dominant culture and will maintain and/or eliminate elements from their culture(s) to function well in these communities or to "live in two worlds" successfully. For years, many Native Americans, including Navajos, have (re)defined and (re)created their identities to survive processes of assimilation and to thrive in spaces of assimilation.

Like other Native Americans, I know what it means to "live in two worlds." I am a subject in the ever-changing world and can assimilate easily to this change. I partake in various discourse communities; one important one to me is the Navajo Nation, a self-governing community with a collective history, a shared language, and place-based traditions that shape Navajo culture and philosophies. I identify as a Diné Asdzáán or a Navajo woman because I belong to four different clans: my mother's maternal clan, my father's maternal clan, my mother's paternal clan, and my father's paternal clan. When meeting other Navajos for the first time, I would identify myself in this way: Na'neeshteezhi Tachine nishłį́. Kiiyaa'áanii báshíshchíín. Honághááhnii dashicheii. Maiideeshgeezhnii ei dashinali. Na'ni ahdi ayisi dashighan. Akweet'a Diné Asdzáán nishłį́. Here is my English translation: I am Charcoal Streaked People (Division of the Red Running Into Water Clan). I am born for Towering House People. My maternal grandfather is the One Who Walks Around and my paternal grandfather is Coyote Pass People. I am originally from Querino Canyon, Arizona. This is how I identify as a Navajo woman. The intention of this traditional Navajo greeting is to reveal my clans to other Navajos and to identify where I come from. Sharing clans allows Navajos to recognize one another as Diné (Navajo) and to acknowledge any clan relation. When a Navajo person learns that they have the same clan with another person, they will acknowledge the relationship from that moment forward. It is common for Navajos to immediately recognize someone as kin and to refer to them by that established relationship. Navajos who live off the Navajo reservation can identify as a member of the Navajo Nation because of their clan affiliation. In this sense, we are always connected to one another. My clans remind me that I am a part of a larger body of people and have many relatives. When I am removed from my community, I may introduce myself in this manner to non-Navajos to show that I am aware that my worldview is informed by traditions and teachings specific to the Navajo community. It is also a strong reminder that I can draw from and teach the knowledge of my ancestors.

Contact between the Navajos and the United States began in the mid-1800s when the federal government worked to remove Navajos from their tribal lands under a removal policy that would make land available for westward-moving Anglo settlers. In 1863, under the command of General James Henry Carleton, Colonel Christopher "Kit" Carson led a large group of soldiers to round up thousands of Navajo people to relocate them to reserved lands with the hope to also find gold and silver. Most Navajos submitted to the removal process for fear of losing their lives. They were herded to the Bosque Redondo Reservation (Fort Sumner) in New Mexico. Incarcerating thousands of Navajos on the reserve created a financial toll that led to the negotiations of the peace treaty between the United States and the Navajo Tribe, which became known as the Navajo Treaty of 1868. The treaty allowed Navajos to return home. The Treaty of 1868 also required Navajo children between the ages of six and sixteen to attend English education schools. Navajo parents sent their children to schools and accepted the educational and assimilative practices.

I grew up on the Navajo reservation in a three-bedroom home with my parents and eight other siblings. I am the youngest in my family. We were fortunate compared with other Navajo families because our father was able to secure employment on the reservation as a heavy equipment operator. This meant that, unlike other financial providers on the reservation, he did not have to travel off the reservation for employment. My father's job brought stability, so this meant that our family was able to afford a resource like electricity. I grew up having access to electricity (unlike many other Navajos during that time and even today). However, we did not have running water until I was about fourteen years old. The expense to run plumbing pipes across the rural Navajo Nation was too great. We collected water from a local well in a large metal barrel cart that attached to the back of a pickup truck. Hauling water was a weekly task, but necessary for our survival. We used the water for cooking, cleaning, bathing, feeding livestock, and watering plants. We were always mindful about how we used the water because it was scarce. Growing our own food, including corn, squash, melons, peppers, and potatoes, every year was essential. These large fields determined how my siblings and I spent our childhood and teen years. We spent our summers and early falls tilling the land and planting seeds and the late fall harvesting food. I spent many evenings watering plants with a small watering bucket. I grew up learning that my participation was important to the collective. My father and mother were consistent in doing their share and often reminded us of our chores. If I ever forgot, I had gentle reminders from my father who would tell me that I was "being lazy" when I read books for entertainment instead of contributing. I often read my books when he was not around and on bus rides to and from school. Our parents never encouraged my siblings and I to excel in school. However, we were expected to behave well and pass classes. My parents also encouraged us to seek employment when were able to. When I was fifteen years old, I started working at a local trading post during the summers and after school.

My father's paycheck was our only real source of income, besides my mother's rug weaving. My mother often saved the money she received from selling her rugs for items we needed for school, including clothing, shoes, and other school supplies. When I was a first-year student in high school my vision started to blur. I struggled in classes that year because I could not see well. I knew that it was going to be difficult for my parents to buy me eyeglasses, so I did not tell them until my sophomore year when I noticed a continued decline in my grades. I put off telling them because I knew it would be a financial burden for them. Access to books and academic resources was only available through the public school I attended. However, the public school I attended did not have the resources to prepare me for college. There were times that I used the same outdated textbooks my older siblings used. Moreover, there were no lessons on how to draft an essay in high school English courses. We wrote in journals daily and read short stories and answered questions. This meant that I would not learn what a complete sentence was, let alone a fragment or a fused sentence.

When I arrived at the university as a first-year undergraduate student, I realized that I lacked skills and knowledge in writing essays. As a first-generation college student, it was difficult to select a major because I was ill informed about such matters. It took an entire year to grow accustomed to university life, and it would reflect in my grades. While I was earning A's as a high school student, I was earning C's in college. I worked part time as a customer service representative to make ends meet. It was nearly impossible to work part time and be a successful full-time college student. I crammed my way through every test as an undergraduate. I was not proud of how I was doing in college, but I knew I was determined to attain a degree. In addition, it was painful to see the endless resources and support my college roommates had when I often worried if I would have enough to eat each week. This prompted me to secure loans. Poverty was not my only challenge as a student; I grew up in a home where Navajo was the prominent language spoken.

Consequently, Navajo is my first and second language. Today, I understand the Navajo language well, but I cannot speak it fluently. Even though I am not a fluent speaker of the Navajo language, I claim it as my first language because it is the language of my ancestors, my grandparents, and my parents. It is my birthright and will someday belong to my children, even if they, like me, must learn it as a second language in school. The Navajo language is often secondary in my life because it does not inform my academic or financial success like the English language does. However, I am certain that the Navajo language was the first language that I heard. I imagine that the first words I heard were of my mother saying shí awee' (my child) to me. She sang a lot. Perhaps the first words were Navajo lyrics I heard her sing while still in her womb. My mother, father, and older siblings spoke Navajo in our home. My older siblings also acquired the Navajo language while living in dorms at boarding schools because the children spoke it in their private living quarters. On the other hand, I attended a public school and did not have the same living arrangements and interactions that my older siblings did. The English language had become more prominent in my life by the time I was in elementary school.

Everyone spoke English in my home; however, we did not speak Standard American English. This also meant that I could not build a robust English vocabulary. In fact, when I returned to the reservation to visit my parents as a graduate student, I had to speak a slow-paced, limited form of English and broken forms of Navajo to converse with them. They were bilingual but spoke mainly in Navajo. Their thoughts were shaped by the Navajo language. My mother and father only had an eighth-grade level of English education each and struggled often to hold long conversations with me. I once attempted to confide in my mother about depression, a concept that she did not understand in English. I could not convey the entire concept of depression to her in Navajo, so I made several attempts in English. After a while, she grew frustrated by the inability to understand me. She looked defeated when she told me, "I don't understand what you mean. You should pray about it." I remember the pain and disappointment I felt because I hated seeing her with a look of shame and defeat. I walked away from that exchange realizing how my life was the perfect example of how the efforts to assimilate Natives have impacted the community by creating confusion, contention, and chaos in a family unit. I endured other moments like this with my parents; I wondered sometimes if they knew who I was because we often did not get a chance to have long and clear conversations. I can only wonder now since they are deceased (and have been for over ten years).

In addition to the language barriers, I did not have a single family member whom I could "theorize" with because many of them were disconnected from academia and were focused on pursuing entry-level jobs to make a living. When I was with my siblings (and those assimilated to mainstream values), I found that I could be more at ease. However, I never used the jargon I learned from my advanced education to communicate with them. I spoke a basic form of English. I used common words over complex vocabulary because it would not have been appropriate. I always imagined that there was pressure on me to not appear to be "too educated (or too assimilated)" because it would equate to acting "better" or acting "White." I learned to do this after hearing a variety of negative comments from my Native American peers. I often heard comments and questions about the choice of my major. I heard: "Why would you major in English? Isn't that a major for White people? Why didn't you major in Native American studies?" As I made the long drives home from college, memories of questions and comments like these filled my mind. Because of this, I used Rez slang and accented English forms (that I heard while growing up) to fit in with my family and the community. I never talked about what I was learning in college because I feared that it would create a barrier between us because it could come across as haughtiness or being boastful. I focused on conversations that were relevant to my home community. I felt there was a part of me that did not fit well at home. I would downplay parts of myself during the time I spent with my family or when I was in the Navajo community because I wanted acceptance from them. I became fully aware of when to switch communication codes with different groups.

I spoke slowly or more softly around my parents and other elders in my community because that was how they spoke. The elders in my community appeared to be patient and calm. They focused on the present and seemed content with the state of things. They always had a relaxed demeanor and spoke in almost monotone, not being overly emotional or exaggerated. I always made sure that I gazed away from them and gave them glances instead of prolonged eye contact. Prolonged eye contact is often interpreted by Navajos as aggression and rudeness. To make matters worse, this was the exact opposite of how I was expected to present myself at the universities I attended. There were times that I felt uncomfortable in classrooms and office visits with professors who often spoke with certainty, while gazing directly into my eyes for extended periods of time. I tried to return the same gaze out of respect but have found it quite unsettling.

Over time, I felt more confident in raising the sound level of my voice when I communicated with my college peers. This process took time because I grew up around soft-spoken people. It was inevitable that I would communicate much like them and speak in a lower voice level than my mainstream counterparts. When I finally achieved the skill of projecting my voice, I learned that I had other challenges to face. There were times when I spoke too loudly when I came home from college. I could see my mother wince when I spoke loudly, boastfully, or matter-of-factly to her. The winces were always enough to remind me there were acceptable and unacceptable codes of communication.

I often felt the pressure to be an "expert" in the traditions of my people and to (re)learn the Navajo language to avoid ostracization. It is common for Navajo elders to scold younger generations of Navajos who do not speak the Navajo language fluently or who have not acquired traditional Diné knowledge. Even though many of these elders lived through an era of assimilation efforts and can remember a time when they or their children were forbidden to speak their languages in boarding schools, they often do not blame the loss of Indigenous languages and traditions on the years of imposed assimilation. They will often blame parents for not teaching their children Navajo traditional practices and the Navajo language. Historically, the US government mandated assimilation practices in educational institutions that forced Native American students to speak and write the English language only and punished students for communicating in Indigenous languages. The intention of assimilation polices were to eradicate Indigenous knowledge and practices completely. These efforts resulted in the language loss that is prevalent across Indian country. Despite this loss, Native American nations remain steadfast to ensuring their collective survival by maintaining traditional customs and adopting from the dominant culture to adapt successfully.

Rez English or reservation-derived English is an adaptation of the English and Navajo language. It was (and is) organically created by Navajos who, over time, have infused the English and Navajo languages to create new forms. It can include, but is not limited to, accented English, improper English plural forms, misapplication of past and present, and infusing Navajo words into English sentences and vice versa. One example is that the Navajo language does not have a soft p- sound but does have a b- sound. A Rez English speaker will substitute a b- sound for the p- sound in an English word (if the -p sound is in the middle of a word). For instance, a word like puppy might be pronounced as pubby. This occurs with other English words where the Navajo alphabet and sound system influence how English words are pronounced. Furthermore, dissecting a Navajo word illustrates how interconnection is prevalent in the language and the culture. For example, *shima* is the word for my mother. Shi- on its own means me or my. However, -ma (the noun stem) does not have meaning on its own. One might say, instead, *ama* or *hama* for one's mother. In the Navajo language, it is necessary to identify whose mother a Navajo speaker is referring to. For instance, there is no word for just *mother*. There are words for *your mother*, *my mother*, *their mother*, and *our mother*. It takes two or more words in English to say my mother. In Navajo, it takes one word to capture the concept my mother. Similarly, "Skoden" is printed on a t-shirt that is sold at a local flea market in Gallup, New Mexico. Skoden is the way a Navajo person with accented English might say "let's go then." The English words are compressed (interconnected) to create one word or a concept. Furthermore, some Navajo words are invited into English to create a new word or concept that is derived by infusing the rules of the Navajo and English languages. *Dik'ǫ́ǫ́zh* is the Navajo adjective for salty or bitter. To convert the adjective *dik'ǫ́ǫ́zh* into a noun (or name), a Navajo speaker will add an ii to the end of the adjective to make *dik'ǫ́ǫ́zhii* or a bitter or salty person (a noun) in the Navajo language. However, those who speak Rez English will say *k'ǫ́ǫ́zhy* but will simply mean the adjective form, *dik'ǫ́ǫ́zh*. They are applying English language rules by adding a -y. In English, a speaker can add a -y to salt (a noun) to make the word salty (an adjective). Even though *dik'ǫ́ǫ́zh* is already an adjective in Navajo, Rez English speakers will add the -y to make it into an adjective or a descriptive word, which they will use in conversational English. The way a Rez English speaker might use this in a sentence might be, the pickle is *k'ǫ́ǫ́zhy*. Younger generations of Navajos may deride Rez English forms; however, some are also empowered by the distinctness of Navajo Rez English.

Rez English also includes improper use of plural forms. It is prominent to hear older fluent Navajo speakers describe plural objects and subjects in a singular form (or vice versa) when speaking the English language. This is because the singular and plural forms are different words in the Navajo language. For instance, *hastiin* is a singular man and *hastóí* is the plural form of men. A Rez English speaker might show forms of misapplication of the English suffix -s at the end of English plural words. For example, a Rez English speaker might ask, "How many egg do you have?" Speakers of two or more languages will often confuse, negotiate, and interchange the rules of the two languages. This becomes apparent in how they speak and write in either one of those languages, thus producing a new form of English. Languages that people speak, including Rez English, can reveal aspects of a speaker's worldview and thought processes. This is apparent when dissecting the language alongside the central philosophy of the group of people.

Traditional Navajos perceive the world and its inner workings as cyclical rather than linear and value the interconnectedness of all things. *Sa'ah Naaghaii Bik'eh Hozhoon* (SNBH) is a fundamental philosophy for traditional Navajos. SNBH is achieved through a cyclical path that is guided by the four directions, mnemonic devices, and stories. SNBH is made up of four parts: *Nitsáhákees, Iiná, Nahatá*, and *Siih Hasin*. A figure of these concepts might show a circle marked by four directions that represent each concept. The circle will have a cross in the middle to directly connect each concept to the others at the core, therefore interconnecting all four concepts. SNBH recognizes the interconnectedness and/or interrelatedness of all things. SNBH is the idea that one will walk (or exist) in beauty and harmony as they grow old (or continue through all phases of life). Living to an old age suggests that the aged person was not overcome by bad wind (or evilness). To exist in beauty and harmony is to live without ills or faults—including those caused by the self and others. The "others" include all other life forms on Mother Earth, including the flora, fauna, spiritual deities, and five-fingered Earth surface people. This way of thinking promotes the value of living a long life and supports the idea that old age brings with it experiential knowledge, a sacred knowledge.

Diné still remember and recognize the concept of *Nitsáhákees* (thinking) using Mount Blanca (*Tsisnaajini'*) as a marker, which is a mountain located to the east of what was known as traditional Navajoland. The mountain and white shell are mnemonic devices to remember the concept *Nitsáhákees*. *Nitsáhákees* encapsulates all the notions of the new or beginning, including spring, birth, dawn, and the inception of ideas and thoughts. *Nitsáhákees* takes its place in the east direction because east signifies the beginning for the Navajo people. The sun rises from the east and the dawn greets the Navajo people each day. Similarly, ideas emerge in the mind like a new day. When the idea unfolds into a clear concept, it can be developed. This development or planning stage is marked by the south direction, Mount Taylor (*Tsoodzil*) and blue bead or turquoise. The second stage is *Nahatá* or Planning. After the idea has been properly planned, it can be put into action or implemented. The west direction, the San Francisco Peaks (*Doko'oosliid*), and abalone shell mark the stage of implementation or *Iiná*. After implementation, the idea can be seen, touched, and heard. It can be assessed. The north direction, Mount Hesperus (*Dibé Nitsaa*) or Big Sheep Mountain, and obsidian mark the stage of assurance or *Siih Hasin*.

A person who grew up on the Navajo reservation will have encountered stories, lessons, songs, and ceremonies that reflect *SNBH*. I grew up seeing the world around me as dynamic, or ever changing and ever evolving because these patterns were deeply woven into the everyday practices of the people. For instance, I developed experiential knowledge about the seasons and plant cycles and could easily see the interconnectedness of the cosmos, the physical environment, and my day-to-day existence. I also learned to focus on the interconnectedness of concepts and ideas because stories were often place based or connected to mnemonic devices that were natural structures, like a mountain. As a college student writer, I found concepts that emphasized a fixed perspective, like organization of ideas, to be difficult to comprehend because I could not see when one idea was separate from another. In my mind, most ideas were often tightly intertwined with many other ideas. I found it difficult to determine if I was adding too much to a paragraph because the challenge for me was attempting to compartmentalize one idea from other related ideas. My paragraphs had three or four ideas, which I was not able to recognize as an undergraduate writer. Thankfully, over time (while in graduate school), I was able to sort out my ideas into paragraphs in my essays.

While in graduate school, a college professor of education told me that I had great ideas but needed help with grammar because I had too many fused sentences, misused commas, and sentences written in the passive voice. He suggested that I take an English or composition course to strengthen my writing. I felt overwhelmed by his suggestion but decided that he was correct. The composition course opened a new door for me. Finally, as a graduate student, I learned how to write effective introductions, body paragraphs, and conclusions and recognized the distinctions between a sentence, fragment, and comma splice for the first time. I also realized that I did not learn how to write for the academy in my first-year composition course. This was because I did not have consistent exposure to Standard American English forms. This was a turning point for me. I decided that I wanted to help other Native students become successful writers at the collegiate level. I pursued and earned a master's degree in English. Eventually, at the prompting of two English professors at Northern Arizona University, I applied for doctoral study in English.

Just when I thought that I had become a strong writer, I realized that I still had so much more to learn. Comments about my essays from fellow graduate students and professors often reminded me of my inabilities as a writer. The most damaging comments were those provided by well-meaning professors who imposed their voice, their words, and their concepts to academize my writing. I remember seeing lines drawn across my carefully thought-out sentences. Written above these rejected sentences was a version that revealed the editor's privilege to both Standard American English and to English vocabularies. I realized that I could not develop sentences like theirs because I did not have access to the same vocabularies or the same thought process. There were times that I turned in assignments feeling like I took credit for their work. Moreover, I wondered if these professors enjoyed seeing their own words on paper more than being open minded to the unsophisticated and mundane sentences I created. During those times I often wondered if they recognized that this silenced my authentic voice. It was noticeably clear to me that I could not write like them because I did not have the experiential knowledge they had acquired in their upbringing. I did not have access to the same vocabularies as my peers because I grew up speaking simple English, a broken form of Navajo and Rez English. I did not and could not practice Standard American English in my home because no one in my home used this form. I was not able to see the world like my professors because I was limited to what I had access to.

Drafting stories or writing in a narrative format also impeded the academic writing "skills" I was developing. I did not write stories or poetry for many years after being in an English doctoral program because it was suggested in obvious and subtle ways that there was acceptable and unacceptable writing, and stories were usually deemed as unacceptable by professors in rhetoric and composition programs. Acceptable writing included succinctness, clarity, organization, and advanced vocabulary (often disguised as style). Poetic or nonstandard English forms were not always acceptable in composition writing. Poetry and stories were often identified as artifacts for analysis and not theoretical modes. Because of this, I developed a love-hate relationship with writing. I found myself resisting writing, particularly academic writing, because I knew it would be judged by how closely I aligned to the standard forms of English. I felt coerced into changing my entire voice and perspective, including how I saw the world through language. This meant that I spent hours carefully choosing words, words that I started to believe were superior to other words and words that I had never heard or used before. I had to say things in a way that felt pretentious and inauthentic because I wrote things over and over until I no longer recognized myself in the writing. I felt like my entire doctoral experience was faking my way through writing assignments. To get the superior grades that I desired, I felt like I had to be someone else. I mimicked how others wrote and erased the words I would normally use. My doctoral experience often reminded me of stories about the Native American children at boarding schools who were forced to take new identities; their hair was cut, they were put in uniforms, and given new names. To me, writing for academia was my best rendition of being White. I wrote with the intention of molding myself to fit as perfectly as I could. This, of course, was exhausting. The nonstandard forms of English (or Rez English) that I gleaned over time were not acceptable forms in academia. Even worse, because my thoughts were not in the standard forms of English, my thoughts, too, were not acceptable. I felt like I was in the wrong field and at the wrong institution. My writing "skills" changed over time, but I found myself becoming more silent because I lived in fear that my colleagues would agree that I was not in the right place.

Today, I am a professor of English at the University of New Mexico–Gallup. I instruct students early in the semester that Standard American English is the acceptable form at most universities. I also tell the (hi)stories about how a dominant culture influenced the decisions in academia, including those regarding Standard American English. Second, I teach students to recognize that there are variety of Englishes in America, and that Standard American English is not a better or a more correct form of English, but simply the *acceptable* form in academia. I do this by including texts that reveal the diversity of Englishes. We analyze, understand, and embrace the contradictions and ambiguities, the authentic, in the stories and recognize the beauty and truth in these stories. I hope that students will recognize that their stories, particularly their authentic voices and lived experiences, are significant contributions to this world, no matter what language they use to tell it.

A U T H O R   B I O G R A P H Y

Aretha Matt identifies as Diné. She grew up on the Navajo reservation in a small community called Querino Canyon, Arizona. She is an assistant professor of English at the University of New Mexico–Gallup. She enjoys sharing stories, writing poetry, and teaching first-year writing courses.

Reparations for Native American Tribes?

Jeff Rasley

"Reparations" is a loaded term in the current political climate. Many White people react defensively when the issue is raised for African Americans. Although momentum is building to address the issue, and some state and local governments have taken steps in that direction, the issue of reparations has developed a positive or negative resonance depending on which side of our deeply partisan divide one stands. In my book, *America's Existential Crisis: Our Inherited Obligation to Native Nations*, I propose a way around the partisan divide to deal with the United States' obligation to Native nations without calling for per capita reparations.

The claim made for reparations to African Americans, justified because of the long-term effects of slavery, Jim Crow, and the history of discriminatory treatment, has created an emotionally charged political debate. Proponents and opponents can get passionately worked up just by the mention of the word. It is a difficult issue for multiple reasons. People who identify as African American make up 13.4 percent of the US population. That is about 45 million citizens. What would appropriate reparations be for that many people, and how would the government raise the revenue to pay the total amount? How would qualification for reparations be determined? Would mixed-race Americans qualify? If so, what percentage of one's ancestry would be required to qualify? How would a program for reparations be implemented?

WICAZO SA REVIEW SPRING & FALL 2020

The reaction of many White taxpayers is, "Why should my tax dollars go to paying reparations? My ancestors did not own any slaves." Some White voters will oppose reparations on the grounds that their families have always lived in northern states, and they never benefited from slavery. Should those of us whose ancestors were abolitionists or fought in the Union Army get an exemption from a "reparations tax"? I am not taking a position on the issue, but it seems unlikely that Congress will approve a direct-payment system for reparations to African Americans in the foreseeable future.

I think the issue with respect to Native Americans may be approached in a way that is less politically controversial. First, every resident of the United States who is not of Indigenous ancestry has benefited directly from the genocidal conquest of Native nations. Everyone who does not live on a reservation lives on land that was taken from a Native tribe. That is a historical fact, so non-Native voters cannot reasonably argue that they have received no benefit from the genocidal subjugation of Native tribes. As to implementation, the tribal structure of Native communities ameliorates some of the problems of identifying who would qualify for reparations. Each federally recognized tribe has defined rules for membership. The Bureau of Indian Affairs (BIA) already exists as the federal agency in charge of dealing with "Indian Affairs," so that lessens the problem of bureaucratic implementation. "According to the 2010 Census, 5.2 million people in the United States identified as American Indian and Alaska Native, either alone or in combination with one or more other races. Out of this total, 2.9 million people identified as American Indian and Alaska Native alone" (United States Census Bureau, "2010 Census Briefs," issued January 2012). So the total number of people that might qualify is well under 2 percent of the US population, even if all 5.2 million qualified.

Still, "reparations" of any kind to any minority group is a dirty word to many "red" voters and to some "blue" and unaligned voters. You can imagine conservative pundits and politicians wailing, "Where will it end, if we pay reparations to one group? They will all want to be paid!" Rather than getting sucked into another red/blue divisive political battle by advocating a per capita dollar amount to be paid to Native Americans, the issue can be approached as financing the culturally sensitive development of Native communities. Native nations are recognized under US law as "domestic dependent nations." The United States provides financial aid to other nations all over the globe. Federal, state, and local governments finance and subsidize all sorts of projects for local communities. So, a foreign and domestic aid program should be established to fund infrastructure, education, and economic development within Native nations through their existing tribal structure.

Financing could come from these sources:

1. The BIA establishes a "compensation board" tasked to determine the value of land lost by tribes from unjust and illegal "land grabs."
2. A "foreign and domestic aid fund" is established to pay the amounts of compensation determined by the board. A portion of the needed funds should be paid on a proportional basis by states in which any tribes were forcibly removed from their traditional lands. The federal government should pay the rest.
3. Philanthropic foundations, which issue grants for restorative justice and community development, should be tapped to provide additional funds for cultural recovery initiatives by Native tribes and to help finance development of Native communities.

Why should Native American communities receive the benefit of these sorts of funding? The population of North American Indigenous people was decimated and their way of life was largely destroyed by European and American invasions. Demographers estimate the population of Indigenous people in the Americas declined by 90 percent from 1492 to the modern era. Indigenous people controlled 100 percent of the land that became the United States. They now control about 2 percent. Native people were forced at gunpoint to leave their traditional lands and were imprisoned on reservations under color of law, specifically the 1830 Indian Removal Act. Forced marches, such as the Trail of Tears, resulted in the death by starvation and disease of significant numbers of Native Americans. About 4,000 members of the Creek Nation died on the 1,000-mile trek at gunpoint from Tennessee to Oklahoma. Many Native Americans who resisted removal to reservations were killed during the "Indian Wars." Others were killed for trying to leave the imprisonment of their reservations. Around 300 Sioux were massacred at Wounded Knee, South Dakota, because they left their reservation and some resisted turning their weapons over to the US 7th Cavalry. The decimation of buffalo herds and other animal populations that Native people depended on destroyed the traditional hunter-gatherer way of life of many tribes. Traditional cultural expressions and use of Native languages were suppressed by laws and boarding schools. All of these things perpetrated on Indigenous people add up to genocide against Native Americans. That is why.

Furthermore, according to data from the US Census Bureau cited by Poverty USA, Native Americans have the highest poverty rate among all minority groups. The national poverty rate for Native Americans is 25.4 percent, it is 20.8 percent for African Americans, and it is 17.6 percent among Hispanics. Native Americans also have the worst outcomes on all metrics for measuring standard of living, including life expectancy, infant mortality, general and mental health, suicide, drug and alcohol abuse, educational attainment, and unemployment. Casinos on some reservations have made some individuals wealthy and some tribes are much better off than others, but most of the 326 Indian reservations in the United States are pockets of extreme poverty.

The federal government recently took a significant step in the direction I recommend in *America's Existential Crisis*. President Biden's $1.9 trillion American Rescue Plan Act (ARPA), passed by Congress on March 11, 2021, included the "American Rescue Plan for Native Tribes." A total of $31.2 billion is allocated for spending in various ways to benefit Native Americans, and much of that money is to be paid by the BIA direct to Native nations through their tribal structures. According to news releases issued by the White House and Department of Interior, the American Rescue Plan for Native Tribes "makes a historic investment in Tribal communities, the largest single investment the United States has ever made in Indian country."

ARPA passed the House and Senate along strict party lines. So the Biden administration succeeded in funneling significant dollars to Native communities, but it failed to do so in a way that bridged the partisan divide. I think the American public should and will do more, if the case is cogently argued as fulfilling an inherited debt of the United States, especially if the purpose is to fund needed infrastructure and economic development within our poorest communities. (For what it is worth, there was unanimous agreement among the sixteen students in the class on ethical philanthropy I taught at Butler University last semester that sufficient investment should be made in Native American communities to raise the standard of living to the national average. There was not unanimous agreement that per capita reparations are owed, although a majority supported it.)

Some White people have recognized that an obligation is owed to Native tribes because of historical injustices perpetrated by the US government and its agents since the end of the so-called Indian Wars. The massacre at Wounded Knee Creek on December 29, 1890, effectively ended the resistance of Native tribes to the reservation system imposed on them by the US government and state and local militias. General Nelson A. Miles was commander of all US military forces in the Western Territories when the massacre occurred. Although the battlefield report Miles received blamed the massacre on the Sioux for initiating a fire fight, he conducted an investigation and determined that the US government and private contractors acting as agents for the government were at fault for terrible conditions on the reservations in the Dakotas. He also concluded that the commander on the ground, Colonel James Forsyth, was responsible for the massacre at Wounded

Knee and should be court martialed. Colonel Forsyth was exonerated by a court of inquiry, but General Miles was haunted by the slaughter of unarmed Sioux by US 7th Cavalry troopers. For decades after the massacre, Miles continued to plead for some kind of justice for the Sioux people. The general made this argument in a March 13, 1917, letter:

> The action of the Commanding Officer, in my judgment at the time, and I so reported, was most reprehensible. The disposition of his troops was such that in firing upon the warriors they fired directly towards their own lines and also into the camp of the women and children . . . I have regarded the whole affair as most unjustifiable and worthy of the severest condemnation.
>
> In my opinion, the least the Government can do is to make a suitable recompense to the survivors who are still living for the great injustice that was done them and the serious loss of their relatives and property—and I earnestly recommend that this may be favorably considered by the Department and by Congress and a suitable appropriation be made.

General Miles was not alone in pleading for justice to be done by the government. Other White voices, such as Helen Hunt Jackson in her 1881 book, A Century of Dishonor, made similar demands:

> There is but one hope of righting this wrong. It lies in an appeal to the heart and the conscience of the American people. What the people demand, Congress will do. It has been—to our shame be it spoken—at the demand of part of the people that all these wrongs have been committed, these treaties broken, these robberies done, by the Government . . . What an opportunity for the Congress of 1880 to cover itself with a lustre of glory, as the first to cut short our nation's record of cruelties and perjuries the first to redeem the name of the United States from a century of dishonor.

But demands for justice on behalf of Native tribes, even from a US army general and popular author, were largely ignored. The people living at Wounded Knee and on the Pine Ridge Reservation 130 years after the massacre are the poorest people in this country with the highest rate of unemployment living under the worst conditions with the least opportunities for advancement and the lowest life expectancy. Are we finally ready to heed General Miles's and Ms. Jackson's pleas for justice?

In a few cases, federal courts have found that treaty violations by the US government require compensation. The most significant was the 1980 US Supreme Court ruling in United States v. The Great

WICAZO SA REVIEW   SPRING & FALL 2020

Sioux Nation that the government had breached the 1868 Treaty of Fort Laramie. The Court awarded the Sioux Nation $105 million, plus interest, as compensation for the government's breach of the treaty and the resulting loss of the Black Hills. The Black Hills area of what became South Dakota was the traditional land of the Sioux, and was so recognized in the 1868 treaty. After gold was discovered in the Black Hills, despite the clear terms of the treaty, the US government forced the Sioux onto reservations in the most desolate part of South Dakota, the Badlands.

The legal representatives of the Sioux Nation have declined to accept the money because acceptance of the monetary damages is contingent on releasing the claim for return of the Black Hills to the Sioux people. The money is escrowed in a Bureau of Indian Affairs account accruing interest. The value was around $1.5 billion in 2021. But so far, the controlling elders of the Sioux Nation remain steadfast in their refusal to accept the cash. They are holding out for return of the land and will not release their claim to the Black Hills. That may be a principled stance, but that amount of money could be used for the culturally sensitive development of Sioux communities, which are in dire need.

A 2020 Supreme Court case, *Carpenter v. Murphy*, held that members of tribes charged with crimes committed on "reserved lands" must be tried in federal, not state, court. Mr. Murphy, a member of the Creek Nation, was charged with committing a crime not on a reservation, but in eastern Oklahoma. Most of the eastern half of Oklahoma was supposed to be granted to the Creek Nation as its reservation. But treaty rights to the land were not enforced and the eastern half of Oklahoma was overrun by White settlers in the Oklahoma Land Rush. Eastern Oklahoma, including Tulsa, is occupied by descendents of the settlers, other individuals, local governments, universities, other private institutions, and businesses. Nevertheless, Mr. Murphy's alleged crime was committed on land reserved for the Creek Nation by treaty, so he is entitled to claim his right to be tried in federal, rather than state, court.

The holding in *Carpenter v. Murphy* is important beyond jurisdictional issues because the US Supreme Court determined that land treaties with the Creek Nation were broken. However, the Court has not, and I am sure it will not, order the return of eastern Oklahoma to the Creek Nation. Ordering the return of half of Oklahoma, or all of the Black Hills in the Dakotas, to their earlier occupiers would create incredible disruption and probably a violent reaction. Return of significant areas of their traditional lands to Native tribes is a pipe dream. But given the precedents for recognizing treaty violations and granting compensation, activist lawyers should file cases to demand compensation for all the lands taken from Native tribes through broken treaties. Those monetary awards could help fulfill the need for infrastructural, educational, and economic development in Native communities.

Another recent development, praised by many Native people, was President Biden's appointment of Congresswoman Deb Haaland of New Mexico to be the Secretary of the Department of the Interior. Deb Haaland is a member of the Laguna Pueblo Tribe. The Interior Department oversees the BIA and the management of the nation's natural resources. Ms. Haaland understands Native issues on an existential level. Secretary Haaland has ordered the Bureau of Indian Affairs Office of Justice Services to investigate why so many murders and missing persons cases, especially of young women, in Indian country have been ignored or remain unsolved. She has also ordered an inquiry into the abuse, neglect, and deaths of Indian children at boarding schools that were established to "assimilate" Indian children into the dominant culture. These are important issues that should be addressed in the effort to repair the damage of cultural repression and injustices inflicted on Native people by the US government and White institutions.

One of President Biden's first executive orders was to revoke the permit for the Keystone XL Pipeline and halt its construction. Sioux tribes of the Rosebud Reservation sued the Trump administration to stop construction of the pipeline, which would run from the Canadian border all the way down to the Texas Gulf Coast crossing several reservations and lands sacred to Native tribes. The Biden administration also restored as protected land in the Bears Ears and Grand Staircase-Escalante monuments a vast area that the Trump administration opened up for logging and drilling. The Biden administration suspended all leasing for offshore drilling in the Gulf of Mexico and Alaska waters. That executive order was welcomed by Native people who engage in fishing and traditional whale hunting in those waters. By respecting sacred and traditional tribal lands, the US government will improve relations with Native nations and move the healing process forward.

On an extralegal level, there is a recent trend in the United States toward a deeper sensitivity to the feelings of Native Americans about the use of demeaning representations of American Indians. Within the last few years, the names of popular products and the mascots of sports teams have been changed to end the nonconsensual use of Native American images. The treat that was Eskimo Pie was renamed in 2021 to Edy's Pie. In 2022, the Washington Redskins National Football League team changed its name to the Commanders and the owners of the Cleveland Indians Major League Baseball team changed its name to the Guardians.

There has been real progress in recent years made by the government and people of the United States in facing up to the inherited obligation to Native nations. But the process is not complete. For example, $31.2 billion is a lot of money, but divided equally among the 5.2 million US respondents to the 2010 US Census who self-identified as American Indian, Alaskan Native, or mixed-race Native American, is about $6,000 per person. The average cost of college in the United States is $35,720 per student per year, according to EducationData. Org.

The $31.2 billion, even if wisely invested in infrastructure, education, and economic development in Native communities, will not lift Native communities up to the average standard of living of the rest of the United States. It is quite clear that more investments are required. But will any amount of money pay off the debt the United States owes for what it has done to Native Americans?

This was the response of Nick Tilsen, founder and CEO of NDN Collective, Pine Ridge Indian Reservation, in an April 23, 2021, *NewsHour* interview about the Rescue Plan for Native Tribes:

> *There's really no amount of money that the Congress can appropriate to fix its relationship with Indigenous people.*
>
> *It actually has to change its relationship, because if the federal government changed its relationship to Native people and started focusing on a free and prior informed consent, what would end up happening is the entire relationship with tribal nations and sovereign nations would change, because you would no longer see things like pipelines built through our lands, or extractive industries built through our lands, or decisions made about Indigenous people without our consent.*
>
> *And so I hope that this actually—that this investment begins to open a conversation about entering into a brand-new policy era.*

A new relationship in a new policy era would mean that the cultures of Native nations are fully respected and never again viewed as primitive or inferior to Anglo European White American cultures. The historical injustices suffered by Native people would be addressed openly, honestly, and fairly. With their own people in charge of development projects within Native communities, those communities should eventually be free of dependency on federal and state financial aid. The economies of Native tribes should become developed and diverse enough to be, not just sustainable, but prosperous. That is a vision for Native nations beyond reparations. It is a vision of culturally sensitive community development.

A U T H O R   B I O G R A P H Y

Jeff Rasley is the author of fourteen books and has authored over 80 articles, which have been published in academic and mainstream periodicals, including *Newsweek*, *Chicago Magazine*, *ABA Journal*, *Family Law Review*, and *Friends Journal*. He has appeared as a featured guest on over 150 radio and podcast programs. Jeff is the president of the Basa Village

Foundation, secretary of the Scientech Foundation, board member of the Indianapolis Peace and Justice Center, a trustee of Earlham College, and cofounder of the Jeff and Alicia Rasley Internship Program for the ACLU of Indiana. Jeff is a graduate of the University of Chicago, AB magna cum laude, Phi Beta Kappa, All-Academic All-State Football Team, and letter winner in swimming and football; Indiana University School of Law, JD cum laude, moot court and Indiana Law Review; Christian Theological Seminary, MDiv magna cum laude, co-valedictorian and Faculty Award Scholar. He has been admitted to the Indiana, US District Court, and US Supreme Court bars.

Earthworks Rising: Mound Building in Native Literature and Arts
by Chadwick Allen
University of Minnesota Press, 2022

Jonathan Radocay

Scholarship in Indigenous studies and settler colonial studies has long emphasized how the creation of settler societies has always depended on the elimination, extraction, and annexation of Native worlds. This "colonial restructuring of spaces" (p. 33), as Mishuana Goeman describes it in *Mark My Words: Native Women Mapping Our Nations*, unfolds not just on our lands and on our bodies, but also in the symbolic realm—in the spaces of narrative and representation. Indigenous peoples have always contested and "remapped" these restructurings within Native worldviews, histories, and practices. Engaging these remappings, scholars have increasingly looked to Native concepts of space both to critique colonial forms of (racialized, gendered) spatial domination and to affirm the continuance of these concepts in contemporary Indigenous life. Lisa Brooks, for example, reorganizes histories of literary production and space in the Native northeast around *awikhigawogan*, an Abenaki concept that braids together the activities of writing, mapmaking, and the production of (Native) space. Among other Native spatial concepts, Goeman herself has drawn on the spiraling world of the Mvskoke (Creek) stomp ground in the poetry of Joy Harjo.

In *Earthworks Rising*, Chadwick Allen brilliantly contributes to this body of scholarship by exploring contemporary Indigenous artistic, literary, and performative productions that engage with Indigenous earthworks and earthwork principles. These productions include poetry by Alison Hedge Coke and Margaret Noodin, sculpture art by Jimmie Durham, fiction by Phillip Carroll Morgan and LeAnne Howe, and mixed media art by Alyssa Hinton. Earthwork landforms shape and contour the book's nonlinear, spatial organization too, which draws on the three-worlds theory of the universe shared by many mound-building cultures. Aligned with the above world, part I focuses on engagements with effigy mounds located primarily in the Ohio River Valley. Part II, which aligns with the surface world, covers engagements with platform mounds in Cahokia located in southern Illinois and with mounds in Aztalan in Wisconsin. Lastly, part III, associated with the below world, examines productions that engage with burial mounds.

The range suggested in the book's subtitle—Native literature and arts—dramatically understates its scope and critical practice. *Earthworks Rising* is an incredibly ambitious and wide-ranging text. As much as he painstakingly analyzes a dizzying array of Indigenous and non-Indigenous engagements, Allen prioritizes developing research methods that "think *with, through,* and *among*—the mounds" (p. 8, emphasis original), including those that draw from Allen's own personal encounters; his relationships with Indigenous scholars, activists, and communities; and his lifelong experiences living among the earthworks he examines. *Earthworks Rising* approaches mounds as Indigenous writing, and his innovative methodology combines skillful close reading and visual analysis with personal reflection, site-specific collaboration, and other performative, embodied research practices inspired by Monica Mojica, Howe, and relational anthropologist Mary Weismantel. However, Allen's occasional use of complex numerical descriptions in his otherwise compelling and detailed close readings can at times be disorienting and undermine his attempt to demonstrate an alignment between an engagement's "thematic geometry" (p. 55) and a broader geography of earthworks.

Allen's reading of Hedge Coke's poems "Snake Mound" and "The Mounds" in *Blood Run* (2006) illustrates Allen's original critical practice. Drawing on Gregory Cajete's notion that mathematics play a key role in quantifying and encoding Indigenous knowledge about the world, Allen develops a careful but difficult close reading of Hedge Coke's numerical sequencing and use of space. He argues that throughout *Blood Run* Hedge Coke develops an earthworks poetics that "reveals new ways of seeing and new ways of conceptualizing" (p. 50) the Serpent Mound in the Ohio River Valley. Allen's reading moves beyond the page and considers the possibilities that emerge when the poems are performed, when a reading takes into consideration the "modulations of the performers' voices, expressions, and gestures" as well as "the physical orientations of the performers' bodies in relation to the audience" (p. 59). Allen argues that the embodied performance of Coke's earthwork poetics is crucial to her vision of the "enduring vitality of the mounds" (p. 60) and to their continuing importance in aligning and coordinating Indigenous worlds.

Allen draws a connection between Hedge Coke's poetics and the "embodied research" methods that Mojica and Howe use in their site-specific performance art, which prioritize engaging the mounds physically with their bodies, walking and learning from a particular site's geography. Reading across the methods of these different poetic and performative engagements, Allen employs research principles in Indigenous archaeology developed by Linda Tuhiwai Smith, Joe Watkins, Shawn Wilson, Tara Million, and other Indigenous scholars. These principles conceptualize research at archaeological sites like earthworks within Indigenous philosophies—research as an act of ceremony, the researcher an active participant. Shifting from a removed critical voice, Allen includes his own earthwork engagement and provides a first-person reflection on his own encounter with the Serpent Mound during a trip with Mojica and others. Following the earthwork principles he lays out, Allen "mounds" and layers his scholarly readings with other forms of (embodied, personal) engagement that exceed Western critical practices.

In his analyses, Allen also engages with the history of settler earthworks representations, including those found in popular culture and in anthropology and archaeology scholarship. Allen writes that throughout the colonial history of the United States, these representations have played a significant role in shaping settler perceptions of spatial mastery over Native lands, in developing White supremacist racial hierarchies, and in other settler colonial imaginaries. He argues, for instance, that the settler emphasis on the mysterious origins of Indigenous mounds severs the connection between the mound builders and contemporary Indigenous peoples who have enduring relationships with these places.

Earthworks Rising shows that earthworks continue to be part of the "*living* vocabularies and worldviews" (p. 192, emphasis original) of Indigenous peoples. Mounds remain important conduits of knowledge and sites of "productive return" (p. 231) for many Native nations and communities. Covering an astonishing amount of ground, Allen offers us an Indigenous reading practice that (re)situates earthworks as vital forms of Indigenous knowledge production that continue to shape the Indigenous present and the Indigenous future.

AUTHOR BIOGRAPHY

Jonathan Radocay is a citizen of Cherokee Nation and a PhD candidate in English, with a designated emphasis in Native American studies, at the University of California, Davis. His research explores the intersection of critical Indigenous geographies, modernities, and literary form in Native literatures, print cultures, and storytelling practices. Radocay's dissertation, "Stories in Severalty: Allotment and Indigenous Modernisms," reconsiders the historical framing of allotment and other colonial privatization schemes through an interdisciplinary, community-based study of Indigenous texts that navigate allotment's past, present, and future.

A History of Navajo Nation Education: Disentangling Our Sovereign Body
by Wendy Shelly Greyeyes
University of Arizona Press, 2022

Kelsey Dayle John

Greyeyes starts this book with an example familiar to many community members, which is a collision of interests in a public Diné forum on education. Any Diné person knows and has likely attended one of these forums. This example illustrates an ongoing theme of the book: the intersecting mess of authority that affects the education system and its legacy within the larger context of Native nations and the US government. This book aims to demystify and contextualize one of the longest and most frustrating institutions within the Navajo Nation—education—making an important contribution to the ways that decolonial theory can be put into practice institutionally and politically.

Chapter 1 focuses on the meaning and practice of decolonization within American Indian communities and how this theory might be applied to the particular example of Diné education. I admit that the mess of jurisdictions, agencies, acronyms, and stakeholders was confusing in the beginning. However, I found that Greyeyes purposefully avoided the trap of presenting a tidy timeline of events, which would be a disservice to the complexity.

The most important moment for me in chapter 1 is when she argues that Diné people typically focus on the future and generations to come with the belief that looking to the past is futile and at times violent. Because of this, she explains that her intentional look at history is important for future generations. This chapter also puts the work in conversation within larger fields of decolonial theory citing Sandy Grande's book *Red Pedagogy* in conversation with Marxist and decolonial literature from Franz Fanon to Paulo Freire. This is important because it plants the seed for readers to critique the United States' mission for public education, which stresses training for labor. Not to mention, readers have language to understand the racialization inherent in projects of Indian education.

Chapter 2 focuses on outlining the different actors responsible for education on the Navajo Nation—state, federal, and local. Here Greyeyes describes the original purpose of Diné education as the practice of learning to live in relational harmony to all beings. She then uses a chronological approach to help readers understand the rise of different key players and legislation that determines the current moment. The chronology is also put in conversation with the broader landscape on Indian policy showing that educational policy is never just about the field of education, but related to the overall experience of American Indians in the United States. This shows the potential and impossibility given the Nation's entanglement with the federal government as a "domestic dependent nation," a status that casts a constant shadow on the Nation's enactment of sovereignty.

The following chapter takes a deeper dive into the funding and policy landscape that has shaped the current moment. It begins with a brief mention of off-reservation boarding schools, a legacy, I think, could have been braided into other parts the book since its impact on education continues to be so great. A few important historic moments include the Johnson–O'Malley Act, the Meriam Report, the Kennedy Report, and the No Child Left Behind (NCLB) Act, which all frame the scope of the Diné Department of Education's authority as well as the changing national landscape of educational policy.

Chapter 4 gives a breath of fresh air because it centers the rise of locally controlled schools as the reader begins to understand that "tribal control" is interpreted by many as "localized control." This foregrounds the work at the Low Mountain and Rough Rock schools. I would not say that Indian education began with these schools but that they marked moments where informal education met formalized schooling. This is a distinction mentioned in chapter 2 but is necessary for the reader to remember throughout the entire text.

Chapter 5 further contextualizes the bureaucratic nature of education, explaining how this confusing web of authority came to be. The reader can better understand the goal for the Department of Diné Education (DODE; formerly the Navajo Department of Education, NDOE) to become a state education association (SEA) with more unification and authority. However, this move also brings more central-ized governance to education, giving rise to the conflicts outlined in the final chapters. My hope here is that the reader will use the afore-mentioned theoretical frameworks to pick up on the fact that the NCLB Act (along with other federal policies) renders Indian students invisible and incapable *because of the measures of success* and not only because of the disorienting educational policy.

The final two chapters highlight the ongoing tension between local school boards and the DODE. Greyeyes compares the mission statements of both the DODE and a number of tribally controlled schools finding common ground with Navajo identity and culture, as well as lifelong learning. However, the missions deviate in their men-tion of local communities. Greyeyes suggests that this conflict is cre-ated by the confusing mass of policies, which in many ways forces a stronger oversight by the tribe in order to meet standards and to receive funding.

To illustrate a path forward, Greyeyes shares her findings from interviews with tribal leaders who defined sovereignty in the following ways: home and *k'é*, localized control, tribal government control, full financial autonomy, and the ability to set culturally relevant standards. On the one hand, it seems that the DODE becoming an SEA will solve the problem; however, Greyeyes accounts for the many tensions that result from this path forward. She ends with a smart perspective, writ-ing, "both educational stakeholders need to learn from each other's successes" (p. 177), meaning we can return to our original instruc-tions for education, which is to find harmony within the community and among ourselves. I see this book doing something that other Diné education texts have not attempted to do, disentangling the threads of interest, policy, and jurisdiction within Diné education and providing some considerations for moving forward as a unified community. It is key text for anyone working any part of Diné education.

AUTHOR BIOGRAPHY

Kelsey Dayle John (Diné) is an assistant professor at the University of Arizona with a joint appointment in American Indian studies and gender and women's studies. She studies horse/human relationships in tribal communities with a focus on the social, cultural, and historical narratives of horse/human relations. Previously, Kelsey taught in the Diné studies department at Navajo Technical University on the Navajo Nation. She completed her PhD in Cultural Foundations of Education at Syracuse University. For her dissertation research, she worked in partnership with the Navajo Nation to document horse knowledges and stories for the development of Navajo-centered education and research.

Gichigami Hearts: Stories and Histories from Misaabekong
by Linda LeGarde Grover
University of Minnesota Press, 2021

Katrina M. Phillips

"To live on the shore of Lake Superior," Linda LeGarde Grover writes, "is to live with orientation to water, sky, and forest" (p. 47). *Gichigami Hearts*, Grover's latest collection of stories, poems, and histories, is a beautiful homage to what is now known as the city of Duluth, Minnesota. Incorporated in 1857—a mere three years after the second Treaty of La Pointe ceded most Ojibwe lands in what is now northern Minnesota and a year before Minnesota became a state—the city takes its name from the French explorer Daniel Greysolon, the Sieur du Lhut, who had arrived in the region in the 1670s to set up fur trade routes. Nicknamed the Zenith City in 1868 by Thomas Foster, who started the city's first newspaper, its location at the nose of Lake Superior helped it rise to prominence first in industry and now, among other things, through tourism.

The region's rich Ojibwe history is often obscured, even as its echoes reverberate through the names that dot the city's landscape. The city itself—along with the state of Minnesota—would not exist without the treaty cessions that forced Ojibwe people from their homelands onto smaller reservations, like the ones set forth in the 1854 Treaty of La Pointe. Duluth's oldest social club, for instance, takes its name from *Gichigami*, the Ojibwe name for Lake Superior. Known as *Misaabekong* (the place of the giants) or *Onigamiising* (the place of the small portage) in Ojibwe, the area around Duluth is rooted in Ojibwe history and oral traditions (p. ix). Thus, it is interesting, as Grover muses, that Ojibwe place names are often derived from the physical characteristics of the region, while American place names often draw from a person's name (p. 4).

Like Grover, I am an Ojibwe woman who grew up in the region. The book and the stories within it feel like a homecoming. I know the street names and neighborhood names, I remembered the names of some of the stores and restaurants she references, and I understand the deep meaning Grover places on the stories she tells here. *Gichigami Hearts* is unapologetically hyperlocal, but its reach is far beyond what are now the city limits. It is part history, part autobiography, part geography, and part ethnography, sharing stories of places and people that now might only exist in the collective memories of those who were there or who have since shared these stories.

The book is comprised of four sections: "Point of Rocks," "Gichigami Hearts," "Rabbits in Wintertime," and "Traveling Song." In the first section, Grover intertwines stories from her childhood, her family history, and neighborhood histories into the history of the city's department stores, family-owned businesses, and gospel missions. The second section, "Gichigami Hearts," moves through more stories of Grover's relatives up in Chippewa City, coupled with her tellings of Ojibwe stories of the *mishibizhiig* (the underwater spirit beings of the lake). The stories in the end of this section turn toward the role of Ojibwe people in the tourist trade in northern Minnesota, the people whose handcrafts were sold in tourist stands along the highways that hug the North Shore. Grover places these crafters and entrepreneurs in the long history of Native trade and engagement with Europeans (and, later, Americans), seeking not to denigrate those who sold art to tourists but to understand why and how Ojibwe people participated in these industries. What she calls "the entrepreneurship of Indian stands," she contends, was more than "a crass sale of goods, the desperation of a people in need" (p. 75).

Grover's careful intertwining in and out of these nuances creates a richly powerful story of Ojibwe resilience. Grover weaves Ojibwe history, the histories of treaties and repressive federal policies that aimed to eradicate and erase Native peoples, like allotment and termination, throughout the book. She unflinchingly shows what may have drawn Ojibwe and non-Native men to the missions in Duluth that offered hot food and clean beds in the middle of the twentieth century. She demonstrates the pain and the power of survival. She tells stories of boarding school survivors, of forced removals and migrations, of the Meriam Report and relocation. Grover tells stories that resonate with the readers, and these stories offer a tender manifestation of Ojibwe strength and spirit.

The third section, "Rabbits in Wintertime," more fully centers Ojibwe stories, from the birth of the trickster figure *Nanaboozhoo* and his brother *Ma'ingan*, the wolf, to how *Gaagoons*, the porcupine, got his sharp quills. Grover's "The Harbor: Nanaboozhoo's Brothers of the Heart," a fictional retelling of the Ojibwe winter story of *Nanaboozhoo* and *Ma'ingan*, is heart wrenching and beautifully told. In "Traveling Song," the last section of the book, Grover takes a more redemptive turn, giving the reader an intimate look at the final years of Elias LeGarde, Grover's grandfather. The aching sense of loss that permeates the book—the loss of land and the loss of loved ones—is all too familiar, but Grover's ability to plumb the depths of grief and remind us that the past is, as she writes "always behind the moving, fleeting present," is one of the most moving qualities of the book (p. 140).

There are very few people who could write a book like *Gichigami Hearts*. The sheer range of knowledge Grover explores can only come from someone who has been immersed in the region for decades—and from someone whose familial presence extends far beyond that. If you are looking for a novel, one with a clear beginning, middle, and end, this is not it—and it is likely not meant to be that kind of a book. The subtitle is clear about what this book is, and it is the kind of looping, twisting, circular book that covers decades of stories and histories. It is approachable and welcoming, and the prose is never overwhelming. Grover's explanations of complex federal policies are a gentle nudge toward Native history, and it is an incredible tribute to the past, the present, and the future of the Ojibwe people.

AUTHOR BIOGRAPHY

Katrina M. Phillips (Red Cliff Band of Lake Superior Ojibwe) is an associate professor of Native history and the history of the American West at Macalester College. She is the author of *Staging Indigeneity: Salvage Tourism and the Performance of Native American History* (University of North Carolina Press, 2021). Her current research centers activism, environmentalism, and tourism on and around Red Cliff. You can find her on Twitter @profkphillips.

Hungry Listening: Resonant Theory for Indigenous Sound Studies
by Dylan Robinson
University of Minnesota Press, 2020

Alexa Woloshyn

H*ungry Listening* is a disciplinary reckoning. The book argues that settlers listen to Indigenous music and sounds through settler colonial musical logics. This book has two primary audiences: Indigenous and non-Indigenous. Some of the moments directed to Indigenous readers are open to non-Indigenous readers like myself to witness and learn. Others contain unexplained knowledge or exist in spaces where I am not invited. Robinson also directly asks non-Indigenous readers to name and reject settler logics of listening, composing, performing, and writing. Robinson hopes for transformative intersectional work between Indigenous and non-Indigenous scholars. He models this intersectional work in *Hungry Listening* by drawing on multiple disciplines and speaking to multiple positionalities.

The book title is a concept developed by Robinson, which he explains in the introduction. It is an English translation of two Halq'eméylem words: (1) *shxwelítemelh* ("the adjective for settler or white person's methods/things" [p. 2]), which is based on the word Stó:lō people (xwélmexw) used for starving White settlers in the mid-nineteenth-century gold rush; and (2) *xwélalà:m* (listening). Robinson also provides an overview of his critique of "inclusionary music" and "inclusionary performance" as musical contexts in which Indigenous content is mined for aesthetic interest and "fit"—or assimilated—into

Euro-American classical compositions and performances. Robinson offers an alternative model, "Indigenous + art music," which rejects assimilation and embraces incommensurability.

Chapter 1 introduces the concept of a "tin ear," which reflects the settler listener's ability to perceive only Western ontologies of music. Thus, a "hungry listener" not only desires to consume but also to fit Indigenous content into something knowable and recognizable. Throughout the chapter, Robinson illustrates Indigenous and settler logics of listening. He argues for an unsettling of listening that embraces multisensory, flexible, non-teleological listening and does not appropriate Indigenous ways of listening. Read the introduction and chapter 1 before reading any subsequent chapters, including assigning any later chapters to students.

Chapter 2 models an intersectional citational practice that emphasizes decolonial alliances among Indigenous, Black, Asian, Latinx, settler, and LBGTQ2 scholars. Robinson discusses examples of "performance writing," which he praises for challenging "the unmarked normatively of listening through explicitly marking listening positionality" (p. 81). This chapter challenges music scholars to explore sensory and affective writing approaches that can engage more deeply with our listening experiences. Robinson revisits some familiar musicology texts, asking us to embrace their nonnormative possibilities instead of merely citing them within normative structures.

In chapter 3, Robinson positions his examples—colonial and contemporary—within a four-model taxonomy: integration, nation-to-nation music trading and reciprocal presentation, a combination of the first two, and coexistence without integration. This taxonomy will help analyze case studies beyond those included in *Hungry Listening*. Robinson presents case studies by non-Indigenous composers, in which Indigenous music and stories are forced awkwardly and violently into Western musical structures. In contrast, Mohawk composer Dawn Avery's piece "Sarabande" demonstrates "a sharpness of difference" (p. 143).

Chapter 4 explains how the histories of Indigenous song collection enabled and justified Canadian composers' extraction of Indigenous songs as a resource to create so-called Canadian music. Robinson directs much of this chapter to Indigenous readers with the hopes that they together can find "different means by which [they] . . . might address this misuse of our songs" (p. 151). The chapter ends with a pointed critique of settler imaginings of the Inuit dogsled through an extensive event score for Alexina Louie's *Take the Dog Sled*.

Chapter 5 critiques what Robinson calls "inclusionary performances" for trying to evoke feelings of reconciliation rather than take substantive actions toward nonrepresentational reconciliation. Robinson underlines what is at stake when settler audiences embrace these feelings of reconciliation and do not push deeper: "For settler audience members, it may be a much easier task to embrace the mystery of Indigenous stories and aesthetics than to play a leading role in the eradication of another kind of mystery: the prevailing ignorance of Indigenous histories of colonization and their lasting effects on Indigenous people today" (p. 230).

The book includes several structural challenges to normative structures of academic writing. Robinson engages structural refusal in the section "Writing Indigenous Space," which falls between the introduction and chapter 1. Robinson asks that only Indigenous readers read this section and asks everyone else "to affirm Indigenous sovereignty" (p. 25). As a settler reader, it is valuable to sit with that experience of refusal and reflect: How does it feel not to be invited? Do I believe I should have access to any resource in front of me? Why? If, as a non-Indigenous reader, you are tempted to look through "Writing Indigenous Space," thinking no one will know, stop and reflect on why you would decline Robinson's request. I wish that in the book design, they had left white space opposite the last page of "Writing Indigenous Space." Because chapter 1 begins on the page opposite the last page of "Writing Indigenous Space," even with my firm commitment to not read that section, it can be difficult not to have my eyes fall on the page at all when turning to chapter 1.

Throughout the book, Robinson breaks away from the typical scholarly essay format to offer "written, visual, and aural obstructions" (p. 24). Some of these are small, like the untranslated epigraph on page 25, while others are more extended, such as "Event Score for Guest Listening I." They slow down the kind of hungry listening about which Robinson writes. There are event scores following each chapter. The most extensive is "Event Score for Responsibility" (pp. 191–99), a detailed reimagining of Alexina Louie's *Take the Dog Sled*, including two sets of preperformance instructions and a set of performance instructions.

The final structural intervention is a conclusion that does not emphasize academic work as individualistic and solitary. Instead, Robinson explains that because settlers also need to create their own spaces for working on how to reject hungry listening, he generously makes space for that in his book. So, much of the conclusion is a transcription of an online conversation between scholars Deborah Wong and Ellen Waterman. Robinson enters the conversation later, and the three of them continue to dialogue about the ongoing challenges for all listeners in engaging in this work. Robinson is patient with Wong and Waterman in pointing out the times when they were still hungry for Indigenous labor when they asked him for protocol about their conversation. Robinson responded: "I do think it is necessary that non-Indigenous settler scholars test out and speculate intersectional settler protocol for decolonial listening and writing about music" (p. 252).

The book leaves me with many questions about how I will apply it to my teaching, research, and other musical activities. Robinson has intentionally left that labor to the reader, especially the settler reader. Nonetheless, Robinson employs numerous small and large examples to illustrate both hungry listening and non-hungry listening. This book continuously makes it clear how we are all entangled in hungry listening: we teach it, we write it, and we do it, often without realizing it.

Hungry Listening considers histories, composers, and institutions primarily in Canada. It contextualizes "inclusionary music" within Canada's official multiculturalism policy, and chapter 5, "Feeling Reconciliation," examines performances following the Truth and Reconciliation Commission of Canada. Chapter 1 discusses how the Indian residential schools used sound, music, and language to "fix" the attention of Indigenous children. Many case studies are from composers, performers, and organizations based in Canada. The book's opening critique of R. Murray Schafer likely would be most striking for Canadian readers whose musical education enshrined Schafer's words. Nonetheless, Robinson combines the United States and Canada as lands on which Indigenous people "learned normalized and unmarked forms of settler colonial listening" (p. 3). The commonalities between Canada and the United States make *Hungry Listening* easily applicable to readers in the United States. Thus, I encourage readers to learn more about the histories, treaties, institutions, scholars, and composers specific to the United States and its various regions. Then find ways of applying *Hungry Listening* to a US-based music course, performance initiative, commission, and so on that is relational and respects Indigenous sovereignty in your specific location.

While I would not assign this book directly to students in an undergraduate music history survey, the concept of "Indigenous + art music" and many of the book's examples could and should be part of curricular reform. Listening assignments can be revised to encourage flexible, multilayered listening from students. This book would be appropriate for upper-level undergraduate and graduate sources in sound studies, Canadian music, listening, and dramaturgy. Courses on research and writing about music could focus on chapter 2 and some of the structural interventions Robinson employs, such as the event scores. Chapter 4 would be especially imperative for ethnomusicology and composition seminars.

AUTHOR BIOGRAPHY

Alexa Woloshyn is the Cooper-Siegel Associate Professor of Musicology at Carnegie Mellon University. Her research considers how electronic, physiological, and sociocultural technologies mediate music making and listening. Her book on the Canadian Electronic Ensemble is forthcoming with McGill-Queen's University Press. Woloshyn also researches settler-Indigenous listening encounters and anti-/de-coloniality. Her recent work has been published in *Intersections, Contemporary Music Review,* and the *Journal of Popular Music Studies,* as well as chapters in *The Bloomsbury Handbook of Music Production* and *Popular Music and the Politics of Hope: Queer and Feminist Interventions.* Find her on Twitter @Lexi_LouW.

Red Scare: The State's Indigenous Terrorist
by Joanne Barker
University of California Press, 2021

Kara Roanhorse

US empire defines terrorism as the "unlawful" use of violence, fear, and intimidation, particularly against civilians, in the pursuit of ideological or political aims. The term primarily refers to intentional violence and is used most often in the context of war; however, terror and terrorism in relation to Indigenous people are reproduced differently under the US/Canadian settler empire. What does it mean to call Indigenous people terrorists on their own land? This is a question Lenape feminist Joanne Barker addresses in *Red Scare: The State's Indigenous Terrorist*, noting, "Indigenous People are identified and made identifiable by the state as terrorists in order to advance imperialist objectives" (p. vii). Two defining concepts she uses, the Murderable Indian and the Kinless Indian, are meant to be identifiers for how Indianness is "terrorism" and therefore justifies the genocide and Indigenous removal from their lands. The Indigenous feminist framework which Barker takes up disentangles settler policies, signifiers, and language used for antiterrorist laws and sentiments. Terror and the fear-driving discourses of settler empire reinforce a designation for settler justifications and weaponizing for harsher sentencing of the state's exploitation, policing, and violence under the systems of colonialism and capitalism. In the US and Canadian contexts, terrorism and terrorists are defined exclusively within settler political order. Thus, the "red scare" embodies the full spectrum of settler racism and xenophobic fear that justifies war-making against Indigenous people. The racism and fear further perpetuates into a belief that security and social stability

WICAZO SA REVIEW   SPRING & FALL 2020

requires the extermination or genocide of Indigenous people. This is how they handle the so-called Indian problem. The business of utilizing fear in the name of order against Indigenous people is the basis of settler freedom: figures of terrorism created by state and capitalist industries authoritatively deem Indigenous movements as the ultimate threat to society.

Barker is clear about the realities of contemporary Indigenous struggles like "NoDAPL" (No Dakota Access Pipeline), Wet'suwet'en land defenders, and the Missing and Murdered Indigenous women (MMIW) movement. It is clear how violations of land and territory, the sexual and environmental violence are each intertwined with police violence, prompting many radicals to envision solidarity building as central to the state's historical and political contextualizing of "terrorism" under the US empire's neoliberal state. As Barker illustrates, companies of resource-centered extraction of gas and oil raise questions of identity by intentionally disavowing and challenging Indigenous territorial rights, sovereignty, and self-determination. The militarizing of police and increasing harm to the environment alongside the ongoing MMIW epidemic is why Indigenous feminists' critiques of the state and violence must be concise. Barker's succinct analysis of the political weaponization of identity fraud makes visible the ever-present conflicted and contradictory work of racist ideologies of cultural authenticity and rationalizations of state violence and suppression placed on Indigenous people. Figures of terrorism are made and remade by the United States and Canada to create order whereby Indigenous sovereignty and their movements threaten national security and social stability. Such threats are linked to all manner of protecting settler economic infrastructure and growth at any cost.

Barker first introduces the figure of the "Murderable Indian" as "the first and last authentic Indian," crystalizing how Native people are subjected to a certain kind of criminalization, not just incarceration but of constant surveillance and other types of police violence from the state; they are "an affect of racist fears" and concerns for the settler public and thus require a national security response. The Murderable Indian serves to "license the state's counterterrorist, military, police, and vigilante responses to contain, punish, and deter" (p. vii). Barker asserts this Indian as one that is familiar because they are deemed too much of a threat, whereby the state responds to their terrorism with full force. The Murderable Indian faces the state's counterterrorist measures (including corporate security contractors, invasive surveillance, detention, interrogation, and incarceration), drawing from examples of police violence experienced by water protectors, land defenders, and the work of Indigenous-led movements. Under its own logic, the state being "under attack" has the legal authority to kill Indigenous people and act to utilize and increase lethal forces. Murderable Indians are characterized as "savage" by refusing settler conditions and recognition; they are criminalized for organizing against genocidal policies and upholding Indigenous political governance. This is how they become the ultimate threat to the US empire, enticing corporate security contractors to effectively justify their deployment measures through terror and fear. The intervention made by Barker is this effectivity of terror: the Murderable Indian requires disproportionally more repressive, disciplinary state interventions in order to protect public safety and national security. The effect of terror is deeply racist and requires Barker's analysis not only of the ways identifiers of Indigenous peoples are articulated, but also why Black people, Arab people, Mexican people, and other oppressed people have been deemed so-called terrorists who must be stopped with police and military violence in defense of the state.

Similarly, the "Kinless Indian" enables false and fraudulent claims to Indian ancestry and identity claims premised as an individual claim to property; such claims also "seem to absolve the notion that one might have any benefit from or complicity with the dispossession of and violence against Indigenous people" (p. viii). Barker's term coincides with the politics of recognition and reconciliation for how she scrutinizes the notion of Indigenous identity to go beyond its neoliberal paradigms and toward responsibility and accountability rooted in community. Simultaneously, Barker considers how this Indian provides the state's rationale to aggressively challenge Indigenous people's rights while delegitimizing Indigenous relationalities and ideological notions of dispossession. This figure is an Indian without kin: their self-identification is useful to the state's continued legitimization of racism as justified and the erasure of Indigenous distinctiveness. The Kinless Indian's claims to Indigeneity are fraught for they do not have any lineal or community-based relationships with Indigenous peoples and are misaligned from notions of belonging, kinship responsibilities, and accountability. These individuals are used by the state to challenge Indigenous governments and territorial rights. Different than the Murderable Indian, the Kinless Indian can shift as terrorizing figures to the state when they are seen as threatening the social integrity of the state—they are also direct threats to Indigenous sovereignty. Barker has already argued in *Native Acts: Law, Recognition, and Cultural Authenticity* that the state's Indian (who embodies state-supported values and identity) is embedded in cultural as well as biological notions of racial authenticity that sustain the legal legitimacy of Indigenous rights.

Barker's conclusion gestures toward a future rooted in Indigenous knowledge and understandings for a future that no longer is constrained by the Murderable and Kinless Indians. In Barker's *Critically Sovereign: Indigenous Gender, Sexuality, and Feminist Studies* edited book, she makes similar claims for a queer Indigenous feminist lens to decipher what the state tends to do and will do to Indigenous people, their territories, land, and rights. She is less interested in "futurisms" and more inspired by abolition in the here and now because of what it means to Indigenous people: an end to territorial occupations, carceral systems, police violence, and social institutions that blame incarcerated people for imprisonment. Barker clarifies the concept of Indigenous orientations to the future despite antagonisms with the state. The future is not something we are waiting for, but rather is already embodied in Indigenous relationships with one another in the present. These relationships anticipate the abolition of state imperialism and the already real, existing alternative of Indigenous governance and relationality to imperialism and neoliberalism. The Murderable Indian and Kinless Indian are effective as figures to directly name and call attention to the violence and material conditions of the present, while providing a discursive and ideological realignment of Indigenous opposition to state imperialism. It is imperative to push back against state subject-making—to refuse identifiers and figures—because of the limiting and deadly outcomes, particularly how fraudulent claims to Indianness are bound up in settler discourses privileging the individual and their transgressions. Indigenous opposition calls not merely for the abolition of the state, but also a commitment to Indigenous governance systems based on values of relationality and responsibility—much of what Barker has already said in previous publications.

How do we both disentangle and abolish the entire edifice of terrorism built to protect imperialism and capitalism? While I do not believe this question is one that can be easily answered, we can still name and question what needs to be answered by the prospects and eventuality of abolition. For the earth to survive, Indigenous scholars and feminists attest to the effort to realize what kinship is and means through the lens and politics of queer Indigenous feminism. As Indigenous feminism ethics and relations imply, it is not the work Indigenous peoples must do to "out" frauds or fill in the gaps and silences left in the wake of challenges to Indigenous sovereignty. Rather, our struggles for liberation must continue to be the focal point of our work and we as Indigenous peoples need not be caught up in that sticky and often exhausting work—work that needs to be done in the field and study of Whiteness. Joanne Barker has written and inspired us to believe in relations and kinship as the way forward.

AUTHOR BIOGRAPHY

Kara Roanhorse is a fourth-year PhD student in the Department of American Studies at the University of New Mexico. She is Diné from Tó'hajiilee, New Mexico. Kara is currently working on multiple projects focused on critical Indigenous studies, feminist media critique, queer Indigenous feminisms, and historicizing Native youth liberation movements. Her future dissertation project is interested in the intersections of Indigenous feminist care work, pedagogies of praxis, critical Diné studies, and youth movement building.

Di-bayn-di-zi-win (To Own Ourselves): Embodying Ojibway-Anishinabe Ways
by Jerry Fontaine and Don McCaskill
Dundurn Press, 2022

Sasha Maria Suarez

In a world where the place of Indigenous studies has been, to some extent, accepted within colleges and universities, can we confidently say that this acceptance—or incorporation—is occurring in a meaningful and lasting way? What does it even mean to "incorporate" a field that relies in large part on the use of Indigenous pedagogies, methodologies, ontologies, and epistemologies? Is it a matter of fitting such a field into preexisting colonial institutional structures or must there be a more rigorous process of coming to terms with what it truly means to support Indigenous studies? Can you "indigenize the academy"? Jerry Fontaine (Sagkeeng First Nations) and Don McCaskill take up the above questions in *Di-bayn-di-zi-win (To Own Ourselves): Embodying Ojibway-Anishinabe Ways* and challenge the possibility of incorporating Indigenous epistemologies and ontologies into reconciliation-based efforts promoted by Western institutions of higher learning in Canada.

Di-bayn-di-zi-win is primarily an Anishinabe studies text, one that prioritizes Anishinabe-specific world views and "i-nah-di-zi-win" and "nah-nahn-gah-dah-wayn-ji-gay-win"—Anishinabe ways of knowing and being that are loosely compatible with the concepts of ontology and epistemology (p. 15). Though this monograph does speak broadly to Indigenous studies as a whole and to other Indigenous nations' own ways of knowing or being, it is best approached understanding that not all concepts, pedagogies, or practices described within are translatable with other Indigenous cultures. This is particularly important to note given the extensive use of Anishinabemowin (Anishinabe language) and Anishinabe ceremonies, stories, and practices. Anishinabe is loosely translatable as "human being" and may fit within contemporary concepts such as Indigenous or "Indian," but Anishinabe also contains specific cultural, legal, and political meanings that are not inherently transferable to all Indigenous peoples in North America or elsewhere.

Similarly, the importance of Anishinabemowin, which both Fontaine and McCaskill highlight, requires the reader to consider how the inclusion of language is designed to unsettle expectations of discourse around Indigenization of the academy. However, one should be cautioned against using the language and concepts as broadly applicable in every Indigenous studies case. Although both authors demonstrate the importance of using Indigenous protocols and practices, which include language, *Di-bayn-di-zi-win* is specific to "Anishinabe-Ojibway" practices and attention should be paid to how language is being used both in relation to translatable (and the untranslatable nature of) Anishinabemowin and the use of phonetic orthography in the dialect of Anishinabemowin that Fontaine speaks (which is used extensively throughout this review, though it is not the orthography I am most familiar with).

As is the case with Indigenous studies more broadly, Anishinabe studies is precariously positioned within institutions of higher learning that favor Western systems of knowledge production. Fontaine and McCaskill demonstrate what this precarity has and continues to mean by sharing their own personal experiences with Canadian colleges, universities, governments, and the reconciliation process. Structured within Anishinabe storytelling practices, *Di-bayn-di-zi-win* provides Indigenous and non-Indigenous perspectives on the history of Indigenous studies and the questionable nature of incorporating Anishinabe pedagogies, methodologies, and praxis without truly knowing what they mean and how they are utilized within Anishinabe societies.

A common thread throughout the book is the importance of using Anishinabe "bish-kayn-di-ji-gay-win" (pedagogy) and "i-zhi-chi-gay-win" (methodology) inside and outside of academic spaces to truly grasp what practicing Anishinabe studies means. In the first half of the book, McCaskill utilizes crucial Anishinabe "protocols, principles, and practices" to demonstrate how they "can be the basis of genuine reconciliation and indigenization of the academy" (p. 19). McCaskill, a non-Native person who has decades of experience teaching Indigenous studies and learning Anishinabe worldviews, uses his experiences with Anishinabe pedagogy to articulate how the Canadian state has failed to reconcile Anishinabe practices and pedagogies in the work of reconciliation itself. Using his positionality, McCaskill argues that Indigenizing of the academy must necessarily result in examination of what it means to embrace Indigenous pedagogies within Western institutions of higher learning given long-standing power differentials between Indigenous people and the settler state.

Fontaine builds on McCaskill's writing in the second half of the book by exploring his own perspective, which is shaped by being an Anishinabe man who understands Anishinabe pedagogy as intimately linked to language, story (oral histories, teachings and sacred stories, moral stories and stories of personal experience), and ceremony. Fontaine asks the reader to consider how Anishinabe studies relies on "di-bayn-di-zi-win" (self-determination), which in turn relies on culture, language, and spiritual ways of being that articulate relationality. There is no singular answer to Indigenizing the academy because such a process must start with acknowledging that such a thing cannot be possible without Anishinabe ontologies and epistemologies. Fontaine asserts that Western co-optation of Anishinabe studies through concepts such as Indigenization, reconciliation, and even decolonization demonstrates a potential incompatibility between Anishinabe pedagogies and the academy precisely because the latter does not truly understand holistic Anishinabe worldviews.

What is perhaps most intriguing about *Di-bayn-di-zi-win* are the ways in which the text itself is evidence of praxis and not merely theoretical interrogation. Each author utilizes Anishinabe practices and protocols (e.g., storytelling, prayer, language use) to demonstrate *how* intellectual discourse can be structured in a way that does not overprivilege colonial impositions of knowledge production and practice. By centering Anishinabe ways of being and knowing, this book challenges the current relationship Indigenous studies holds with institutions of higher learning (and colonial societies at large). By examining history, spirituality, and personal experiences, Fontaine and McCaskill present a text that is really about "doing" and "being" rather than solely critiquing or engaging settler colonial institutions and practices. US-based readers have the potential to also gain much from the book because it has clear applicability across colonial borders. Though there are a few things readers will certainly grapple with, *Di-bayn-di-zi-win* offers space to think through the practice, place, and presence of Indigenous lifeways in a manner that could prove beneficial to all.

AUTHOR BIOGRAPHY

Sasha Maria Suarez (direct descendant of the White Earth Ojibwe Nation) is an assistant professor of History and American Indian

Studies at the University of Wisconsin-Madison. She received her PhD in American Studies at the University of Minnesota in 2020 and has published work for the Urban History Association's blog, *The Metropole*, Belt Magazine, and in the recent edited volume, *Indian Cities: Histories of Indigenous Urbanization* (University of Oklahoma Press, 2022).

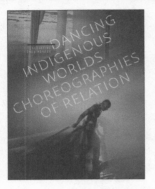

Dancing Indigenous Worlds
Choreographies of Relation
Jacqueline Shea Murphy

"A deeply ethical, deliberate 'witnessing' of Indigenous dance making. There is room for all, and everything, as Jacqueline Shea Murphy reminds us, begins with respect."
—**Michelle Erai**, author of *Girl of New Zealand*

$35.00 paperback | 408 pages

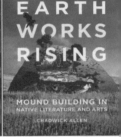

Native Agency
Indians in the Bureau of Indian Affairs
Valerie Lambert

"Details how BIA leaders and employees have transformed a colonial institution through Indigenous creativity and commitment."
—**Philip J. Deloria**, author of *Becoming Mary Sully*

$27.00 paperback | 376 pages
Indigenous Americas Series

Making the Carry
The Lives of John and Tchi-Ki-Wis Linklater
Timothy Cochrane

"A valued contribution to Minnesota's Indigenous history." —**Carl Gawboy**, artist and author

$24.95 paperback | 328 pages

American Indians and the American Dream
Policies, Place, and Property in Minnesota
Kasey R. Keeler

"[Offers] crucial new insights on Indigenous place, space, and suburbanity." —**Daniel M. Cobb**, editor of *Say We Are Nations*

$25.00 paperback | 252 pages

Earthworks Rising
Mound Building in Native Literature and Arts
Chadwick Allen

"Calls attention to earthworks as monumental achievements in science and aesthetics."
—**Wai Chee Dimock**, author of *Weak Planet*

$35.00 paperback | 408 pages
Indigenous Americas Series